Stevie Smith

————————————— * —————————————

A Selection

Stevie Smith

A Selection

Edited by Hermione Lee

faber and faber
LONDON·BOSTON

First published in 1983
by Faber and Faber Limited
3 Queen Square London WC1N 3AU

Photoset by Wilmaset, Birkenhead, Merseyside
Printed in England by Clays Ltd, St Ives plc
All rights reserved

A CIP record for this book
is available from the British Library
and the Library of Congress

ISBN 0-571-13030-5

This selection is for Josie, Clio, and Jason

Contents

*

Contents

Acknowledgements

---- * ----

The editor and publishers are grateful to the following for permission to use Stevie Smith's work in this selection:

Virago Press Limited for 'The Story of a Story', 'Syler's Green', 'Cats in Colour', 'My Muse', and 'What Poems Are Made Of', all taken from *Me Again: Uncollected Writings of Stevie Smith*; also for the excerpts from the three novels, *Novel on Yellow Paper*, *Over the Frontier*, and *The Holiday*, all available in Virago Modern Classics. The extracts in 'On Writing' are taken from the novels, from *Me Again*, and from *Ivy and Stevie* by Kay Dick, published by Duckworth.

The poems are taken from *The Collected Poems of Stevie Smith*, by courtesy of the publishers, Allen Lane and Penguin Books, Ltd., and by permission of James MacGibbon. In a very few instances, this edition adopts variants introduced by Stevie Smith in her selections of 1962 and 1966. The poems are arranged here under the titles of the volumes in which they were originally published. The titles for the selections from the novels are the editor's.

The editor is personally grateful to John Barnard, Josephine Lee and Christopher Ricks for their help and advice and to James MacGibbon for his enthusiasm and benevolence.

Preface

————————— ✳ —————————

As Stevie Smith's executor I have had the privilege of watching
from a front seat in the stalls, so to speak, her growing popularity.
When she died in 1971, in her sixty-ninth year, she had been
recognized in literary circles as a poet with a unique talent. Sir
Desmond MacCarthy, the doyen of the critics in his day who
belonged to a generation older than hers, had written some
twenty years earlier that she possessed 'a little nugget of genius';
in 1969, on the recommendation of C. Day Lewis, then Poet
Laureate, she was awarded the Queen's Medal for Poetry, and
when she died she was acclaimed by her contemporaries and the
younger critics as one of the most original poets of our time. That,
as it has turned out, was only the beginning of what is proving to
be her remarkable posthumous celebrity.

Stevie's work is now being read no longer just in the United
Kingdom but across the world, in English and in translation, in
Japan, in the Continent of Europe and, above all, in the United
States of America, where she had only slight success in her
lifetime. She must be among the most frequently anthologized
poets in English-speaking countries; and, to judge by the number
of letters I get from schools, she is beginning to be widely read by
teenagers. Hugh Whitemore's play and film, in which Glenda
Jackson played the title roles, have no doubt fanned this fire of
interest, but they cannot be the whole cause of it.

Great as Stevie's popularity now is, I doubt if all of her new
public appreciate her poetry to the full. Many of her admirers are
still inclined to regard her as an eccentric writer of light verse with
a wry, even sick, sense of the absurd, and that is why it is so
gratifying that Hermione Lee has put things right. The poems
and prose passages she has chosen for students offer a
representative range of Stevie's work in all its varied moods; and
the insight of her Introduction and her placing of the poet in the
English literary tradition (I found her comparison of Stevie with
other poets particularly helpful) all contribute to making her book
an inviting overture to the entire opus of 'one of the most original
poets of our time'.

James MacGibbon

Introduction

'Remember life not to cling to it,' says Father Whatshisname to the lady in her cell.

> Well I don't you know, said the lady, then aware of
>   something comical
> Shot him a look that made him feel uncomfortable.

Like much of Stevie Smith's work, this poem ('The Hostage') makes a reasoned, humorous, and dignified case for welcoming Death, as Seneca and the Stoics did. But it is a useful starting point in other ways, too. The lady's unexplained dramatic situation ('You hang at dawn, they said') is one of many mysterious journeys, fatal or fortunate quests, in Stevie Smith's poems and fictions. Her characters are perpetually saying goodbye to their friends, riding away on dangerous missions, like Browning's Childe Roland, or getting lost in a blue light or a dark wood. One 'lady' is swept off by her huge hat on to a 'peculiar island'; others are magicked out of the real world into a Turner painting, or into the domain of a river-god or of 'the lady of the Well-spring'. The hostage's reasons for wanting to die, and her quizzical reception of Father W.'s well-meant Christian consolations, are quite as characteristic. Stevie Smith is childish, whimsical, fantastical, escapist; she is, equally, tough, pragmatic, satirical (especially of 'the Christian solution' and of the English middle classes to whom she belongs) and intellectually rigorous. Her tone of voice, at once alarming and domesticated, combines these two sides. In the two lines from 'The Hostage', the lady's flat, matter-of-fact colloquial remark, the long, chatty, narrative line, and the purposely obtrusive half-rhyme give an effect at once comical and uncomfortable. Her poems all shoot us this sort of look, and make us 'aware of something comical' going on. They are about feeling funny, and they give us funny feelings.

'The Hostage' is typical, too, in being a conversation piece, in which the lady makes her confession to the priest. Seamus Heaney has called Stevie Smith 'a memorable voice', meaning not only that her own reading voice affected his response to her poems, but also that they are 'poems of the ear'. They make us aware of a relationship between 'a speaking voice, a literary voice (or style) and a style of speech shared by and typical of a certain social and cultural grouping'—that is, the educated English middle classes. An idiosyncratic speaking voice that accosts the reader, a voice of a particular class, speaking with what Heaney calls the accents of 'disenchanted gentility'—as though the Ancient Mariner had taken up residence in Palmers Green—is, certainly, the most striking quality (and not just of the poems: 'This is the talking voice that runs on', says the narrator of *Novel on Yellow Paper*). And all kinds of 'speaking' are found in the poems: letters, confessions, prayers, songs, messenger speeches, dramatic monologues, addresses, advice-columns, conversations (some rather one-sided, like 'The After-thought'), Socratic dialogues, debates and arguments. Invocations are frequent: 'Away, melancholy', 'Do take Muriel out', 'Honour and magnify this man of men', 'Girls!', 'Reader before you condemn, pause', 'Crop, spirit, crop thy stony pasture!', 'Farewell, dear friends', and (most of all) 'Come, Death'.

This talking voice sounds simple and spontaneous, but is more cunning than it seems. Stevie Smith's manner can be baffling; at times, as D. J. Enright says, one simply asks: 'So what?' The zany, scatty, somewhat Thurberesque illustrations, the eccentric reading manner—she would sing her poems off-key, or recite them in a rather childish voice—the cryptic off-hand oddity of some of the shorter poems, invite dismissive words like 'batty' and 'fey'. Her early reviews were condescending ('Miss Smith is carrying her individuality and eccentricity further than ever', *Times Literary Supplement*, April 1943; 'Does Miss Smith mean herself to be taken seriously?' *Times Literary Supplement*, December 1950; 'As with Ogden Nash, a small amount goes a long way toward being enough', *Poetry*, August 1958). Her reputation grew during the sixties and seventies, and since her death in 1971, Virago's reissuing of all the prose has ensured that she is taken seriously. The other tribute to her popularity, Hugh Whitemore's play (and film) *Stevie*, unfortunately laid the emphasis on the dotty spinster of Palmers Green, all funny hats and pussy cats. The suspicion that she is an over-rated minor English comic writer is likely to persist; Stevie Smith is a riddler, and has concealed her own complexity. Her fictional heroines' favourite pursuit is unravelling codes and ciphers, and she likes riddle poems ('The Ambassador'), or gnomic verses which can't be understood without their illustrations ('The Rehearsal', 'The Persian'). The larger riddle, however, is how her 'naïve' effects are produced.

She has, to begin with, a very sophisticated and exact sense of line. This can take the form of strong hymn and ballad metres ('To the Tune of the Coventry Carol', 'The Lads of the Village', 'At School', 'Nor We Of Her To Him') or of experiments with a range of metrical forms. She writes in hendecasyllables (p. 182), in iambic pentameter ('Great Unaffected Vampires and the Moon'), in the eight-stress trochaic tetrameter of Tennyson's 'Locksley Hall' ('The Airy Christ'), or in firm seven or four stress lines ('Anger's Freeing Power' has both). Some poems will infiltrate a strong regular metre into a free running line (as in the second verse of 'Thoughts about the Person from Porlock'); some will change their tune by abandoning a regular metre in the last line ('To a Dead Vole', 'O Happy Dogs of England').

The long conversational line of many of the poems ('The Hostage', 'The Deserter', 'The After-thought' among others) is not as casual as it looks. The rhythms of speech are carefully played into the lines:

> Marriage? Out of the question. Well for instance
> It might be infectious, this malaise of mine . . .
>
> (p. 137)

as is the sense of physical movement:

> As Red and Honey push by,
> The old dogs,
> Gone away, gone hunting by the marsh bogs.
>
> (p. 146)

> I can hear Arthur roaming overhead
>
> He loves to roam
> Thank heavens he has plenty of space to roam in
> (pp. 162–3)

The line-endings create suspense and surprise, or a sense of enchanted stasis, like the river-god's

> Hi yih, do not let her
> Go. There is no one on earth who does not forget her
> Now.
>
> (p. 113)

or Persephone's

> Oh do not fret me
> Mother, let me
> Stay, forget me.
> (p. 115)

Eve and Mary's argument in 'A Dream of Comparison' is
established by such suspensions:

> 'Oh to be Nothing,' said Eve, 'oh for a
> Cessation of consciousness . . .'

> Mary laughed: 'I love Life . . .
> That's a feeling, you say? I will find
> A reason for it.'
>   (pp. 131–2)

The patient's longing for oblivion in 'The Doctor' is felt through
the running-on of her lines:

>   give me some bromide
> And then I will go away for a long time and hide
> Somewhere on the seashore where the tide

> Coming upon me when I am asleep shall cover
> Me . . .
>   (p. 67)

The transformation of 'The House of Over-Dew' from story to
poem ('If it doesn't fall into verse I'm going to help it') shows the
creation of this 'casual' line, with its hiatuses and subdued
climaxes.

> But, oh, when Cynthia heard that word it was the knell to all
> her life and love. This, she said, is the end of happy days and
> the beginning of calamity. *Over-Dew*, she thought, shall be the
> death of my love, and the death of life. For to that tune, she
> thought, shall come up a European war and personal defeat.
>   (*The Holiday*, p. 178)

In verse this becomes:

> But oh when Cynthia heard that word
> It was the knell
> Of all her life and love. This, she said,
> Is the end of happy days, and the beginning

Of calamity. Over-Dew, she thought,
Shall be the death of my love and the death of life.
For to that tune, she thought,
Shall come up a European war and personal defeat.

(p. 178)

The 'free' conversational line is buttressed from within by the use
of internal rhymes ('The gray of this heavy day/Makes the green
of the trees' leaves and the grass brighter', p. 146), alliteration
('salt silt', 'reverent reveries', 'fuel fed fire'), startlingly
concentrated monosyllables ('Ah, croaked/The door-set crone,
Sun's cloaked', p. 114) and the repetition of simple key words:
'farewell', 'happy', 'glad', 'tender', 'blue'. Rhyme is her most
pronounced device for controlling the line, her favourite kind of
joke, and one of her most cunning skills. The rhymes are often
purposely unpoetical, McGonagall-ish, or Byronesque: ortho-
dox/shut in a box, praevalebit/in a bit, lent a/magenta,
hittapotamus/lost in the fuss, ill-fed/Wilfred, benison/to go on.
This flat-flooted comical perversity, which manages to combine
despair and high spirits in a quizzical, shrugging way, frequently
shades into something sinister, delicate or haunting, like the
rhyme of 'curlews' and 'purlieus' in 'The Magic Morning', of
'mother' and 'smother' in 'Persephone', of 'phantoms' and
'tantrums' in 'Le Majeur Ydow', or the half-rhyme of 'East' and
'Christ' in 'The Airy Christ'. The poems are full of these elegant,
mournful half-rhymes:

There is an island in the lake, old brick walled,
Where the laurestina climbs and is not spoiled.

(p. 87)

All her friends are gone
And she is alone

(p.116)

And they talked until nightfall,
But the difference between them was radical.

(p. 132)

I am happy, I like the life,
Can swim for many a mile
(When I have hopped to the river)
And am for ever agile.

(p. 158)

Her rapid changes in tone, from the maladroit and whimsical to the lyrical, from the *faux-naïf* to the artful, from the flat and gauche to the resonant, are brought about partly by that mastery of line and rhyme, and partly by an extraordinarily heterogeneous diction. Stevie Smith's poems mix biblical archaisms with genteel suburban clichés, ornate Latinate vocabulary (she loves polysyllabic rhymes like inclement/convenient, temporization/indignation, felicity/sufficiency, consideration/realization/preoccupation) with the most matter-of-fact Anglo-Saxon bathos, (words like 'glum' and 'plod'), invocations to Death and the Lamb of God with silly names like Mr Over or Lady 'Rogue' Singleton. Poems such as 'Aubade', 'A Humane Materialist . . .', 'The Recluse', and 'Great Unaffected Vampires and the Moon', are lush and clotted with poetic diction. More often, such language will jostle with commonplace, reductive, colloquial idioms (see, for instance, 'My Hat', 'The After-thought' and 'Dido's Farewell to Aeneas') which may themselves take on a peculiar suggestiveness. The not-quite-romantic wan swan 'On the lake/Like a cake/Of soap': the bodies in the cemetery made more gruesome because they 'have that look of a cheese do you know sour-sweet/You can smell their feet'; the sinister perkiness of phrases in 'The River God' like 'contrary to rules' or 'plenty of go'; the desolating use of 'larking' in 'Not Waving but Drowning'; the ordinary, polite beginning of 'Do Take Muriel Out'; Guinevere's cosy 'where are you dear?' in the strange uncosy 'The Blue from Heaven': these are examples of the arresting effects of this mixture of idioms:

> (I often wonder what it will be like
> To have one's soul required of one
> But all I can think of is the Out-Patients' Department—
> 'Are you Mrs Briggs, dear?'
> No, I am Scorpion.)
>
> (p. 169)

Stevie Smith often uses the word 'peculiar', and it is the best word with which to describe her effects.

Though her voice is always recognizable for its peculiarities, it is much given to doing impersonations. Occasionally these move into another 'social grouping' ('Proper done out of 'er rights, she was, a b. shame', p. 164) but mostly they are middle-class characterizations, like the smug, huffy professional invalid in 'The Deserter':

And every morning the doctor comes and lances my
   tuberculous glands.
He says he does nothing of the sort, but I have my own
   feelings about that,
And what they are if you don't mind I shall continue to keep
   under my hat.

(p. 120)

or the malevolent suburban gossip of 'Emily writes such a good
letter':

> Yes, I remember Maurice very well
> Fancy getting married at his age
> *She* must be a fool

(p. 163)

The novels and stories, though dominated by 'the talking voice
that runs on', are full of people very vividly characterized by their
speech. There are the fearsome upper-class children in
Kensington Gardens (p. 105); or (also in *The Holiday*) Clem, the
malicious rich homosexual socialist whose sayings include 'My
little brother is a carpet-communist', or 'She is a most remarkable
woman, she has tired out three riding horses before breakfast', or
(of the countryside) 'One always comes back to the English
school'; or the nagging husband in the story 'Sunday at Home':

> 'All I ask', sang out Ivor, 'is a little peace and quiet; an agreeable
> wife, a wife who is pleasant to my friends; one who
> occasionally has the room swept, the breakfast prepared, and
> the expensive bric-a-brac of our cultivated landlord—*dusted*. I
> am after all a fairly easy fellow.'

(*Me Again*, p. 44)

Most of the fictional voices are based on Stevie Smith's friends
and enemies (George Orwell, for instance, was split into two of
the characters in *The Holiday*, Basil and Tengal). These
impersonations were so sharply done as, on occasion, to get her
into the kind of trouble that is described in 'The Story of a Story'.

The pleasure in satirical characterizations goes with a relish for
parody, imitation and pastiche. As my notes to this edition show,
Stevie Smith is a highly literary and referential writer, and one of
the peculiarities of her style is the way she infiltrates other voices
into her own. Such references range from the ostentatious and
insistent to the oblique and concealed. (They range, too, from the

accurate to the purposely inaccurate: see my notes to 'God and the Devil', 'Old Ghosts', '. . . and the clouds return after the rain', and 'Phèdre'). Some of her best poems are translations ('Dido's Farewell to Aeneas', 'Songe D'Athalie') or free renderings ('Dear Little Sirmio'). Many of them evoke a particular manner or vocabulary, or mix up several at once: 'Our Bog is Dood' and 'One of Many' are extraordinary amalgams of Blake, Hardy, Lewis Carroll and Wordsworth. One of a generation which learned poetry by heart at school, and which knew the Bible and the Classics well, Stevie Smith's mind is a 'rag-bag' of quotations. In an essay on her schooldays, she gives a list of the poems she heard young, which include 'The Ancient Mariner', Tennyson's 'Ulysses', some Milton, *Childe Roland to the Dark Tower Came*, and a good deal of seventeenth-century religious poetry. In her own selection of verse for children, she expresses a preference for 'fiercer' poems, and includes long extracts from the Book of Job, and a great deal of Romantic poetry (Shelley's 'Ozymandias' and parts of 'The Masque of Anarchy', Keats's passage on Isabella's proud brothers, Byron's 'beautifully *ratty* lines to Caroline Lamb', and Blake's 'The Sick Rose', 'Gnomic Verses', and parts of *Auguries of Innocence*). Among seventeenth-century poems she chooses Southwell's 'The Burning Babe' and parts of Crashaw's 'Office of the Holy Cross' (from which she often quotes). Her nineteenth-century poems show a liking for the grotesque (Tennyson's 'The Kraken', Melville's 'The Maldive Shark', Poe's 'Annabel Lee') and the heroic (Macaulay's *Lays of Ancient Rome*). There is very little modern poetry: Yeats's 'Two Songs of a Fool', Edward Thomas's 'Adlestrop', Frost's 'Acquainted with the Night', and some of her own.

Stevie Smith is often compared to Blake, sometimes to Edward Lear (Heaney says 'she reminds you of two Lears', the suffering king and the nonsense poet), sometimes to Emily Dickinson. Her fondness for hymns, fairy stories, and nursery rhymes is evident. There are also very marked echoes of the religious poetry heard at school (Crashaw, Herbert, Phineas Fletcher) and of Victorian poets, especially Tennyson and Browning. Mixed with this strong attachment to the English tradition, there is a powerful feeling for Greek and French classical tragedy, for Virgil, Homer, Catullus, Plotinus and Seneca, for the liturgy and the Book of Common Prayer.

Her writing is full of these voices, but their use is complex. The paradox of her art is that it is at once so allusive and so idiosyncratic. Other people's phrases become her own:

> ... we do not wish to understand ... it is for us somebody else's cup of tea that we do not even say: May it pass from us. ...
>
> (p. 59)

> I regard them as a contribution to almighty Truth, magna est veritas et praevalebit,
> Agreeing with that Latin writer, Great is Truth and will prevail in a bit.
>
> (p. 148)

More than direct translation or quotation, she likes half-echoes, reminders, re-workings, travesties. A poem such as 'Old Ghosts' or 'A Dream of Comparison' may be sparked off by a passage from de Quincey or Milton; or a story or poem may be written out of a general feeling for another writer. In this way 'Little Boy Lost' is Blakean, 'The House of Over-Dew' is Tennysonian. She likes to make comically casual, fleeting allusions: 'The funeral paths are hung with snow/About the graves the mourners go' (p. 45) calls up Housman's 'About the woodlands I will go/To see the cherry hung with snow'. 'Cold as no love, and wild with all negation——/Oh Death in Life, the lack of animation' (p. 81) invokes Tennyson's 'Deep as first love, and wild with all regret:/Oh Death in life, the days that are no more'. More elusively, the *tone* of a poet may be evoked. There are shades of *Childe Roland* in 'the crescent moon/Performed a devil's purpose for she shewed/The earth a-heap where smooth it should have lain' (p. 143) and an echo of Tennyson (particularly of 'The Poet's Mind' and 'A Spirit Haunts the Year's Last Hours') in 'My soul within the shades of night/Like a languid plant with a fungoid blight' (p. 89).

Some poems rework whole plays and legends ('Phèdre', 'Persephone', 'The After-thought'), or make play with a well-known anecdote, such as Coleridge's being interrupted in the middle of writing 'Kubla Khan' by a person from Porlock. In her prose she will often retell stories—Euripides' *Bacchae* or a Grimm fairy-tale in *Novel on Yellow Paper*, a life of Boethius in *The Holiday*. She parodies tones of voice: a condescending Church of England vicar, or a self-important literary man, or the blushful, hectoring Miss Hogmanimy, lecturing to schoolgirls on purity and abstinence. In *Over the Frontier* Pompey has to listen to a bad-tempered academic reading Pater's description of the Mona Lisa: 'the too-ripeness, the concealed verse forms . . . the dying fall at the end of each paragraph' (see pp. 62–3). Stevie Smith's own voice (itself much given to mingling prose with verse) brilliantly catches the cadence of that sensitive, pulsating, closeted, Anglo-Catholic aestheticism she so fiercely dislikes.

Pompey listening furiously to Pater's dying falls consoles herself inwardly with a satirical line from Juvenal, whom she calls 'a greater than Pater'. Classical rigour set against narcissism, neurosis, melancholia, is the key to her work. D. J. Enright (referring to her preference for Racine because he is more 'truly Greek' than Euripides) says that Stevie Smith's poetry is itself 'somewhat Greek'—'severe, austere, simple, bracing, impersonal'—and goes on to describe her thumping, perverse off-rhymes, her wariness of love and Christianity, her Blakean realism, her stoicism, as 'an avoidance of the romantic'. But Stevie Smith's classicism is coloured by what it criticizes. Her thoughts, like her style, play with contraries: Christianity and paganism, religious fanaticism and the rational intellect, domesticity and loneliness, lassitude and energy, sentimentality and severity, power and escape, human possessiveness and animal (or natural) aloofness, illusions and disenchantment, giving up and going on, love of life and hopes of death. These are not straightforward alternatives. She is, for instance, strongly attracted to 'the Christian solution' (see 'How Do You See?') and has to reason herself out of its dangerous fairy-tale consolations. (Her attempt at compromise is to call herself a 'neo-Platonic Christian'.) Her writing is suffused with 'loamish Victorian melancholy', with tears, longings for oblivion, nostalgia for childhood, quite as much as with classical severity. And her classicism is gothic and barbarous rather than Olympian and serene: she likes best the sinister terrors of Dionysus, or the story in the *Iliad* of the shades who must drink blood before they can speak, or the prayer of the Roman soldiers who devoted themselves to death in battle. Her Persephone prefers the dark underworld (as well as wanting to get away from mother). 'Pompey Casmilus', the name of the heroine in *Novel on Yellow Paper* and *Over the Frontier*, refers us to the 'ambassador' of the gods and the patron of poets, thieves and merchants, and, primarily, to the god who conducted souls to the underworld.

The Holiday (which Stevie Smith thought of calling 'Death and the Girl') perfectly displays this mixture of classical severity and tearful Victorian neurosis. Celia and her cousin, who takes the name 'Casmilus' here, are like Persephone and Pluto, and the landscape of their holiday seems to be the landscape of the underworld. But Casmilus tells Celia that she has 'a romantic feeling for Death', and at one point she floats down the Lincolnshire river like Millais' Ophelia. Her satirical fierceness about post-war England is mingled with a nervous confusion: 'Everything is in fits and splinters'. 'The House of Over-Dew', which appears as a story in *The Holiday*, a dreadful tale of gloomy English Christianity and lost love, grafts a classical idea of fatality and stoicism on to a murky Victorian setting.

The stories Stevie Smith chooses to tell are not as simple, or as playful, as they may look. Certainly her enchanted characters prefer being lost or spellbound to being at home. Persephone likes the wintriness, the 'little boy lost' would be happy without 'father, mother, home' if he could find some food (but he will die of cold and hunger), the girl swept away by her hat will not be taking it off ('Go home, you see, well I wouldn't run a risk like that'), Arthur rides off into the 'blue light/Of the peculiar towering cornflowers', gladly saying goodbye to Guinevere and his throne, and the morbid girl from the office who disappears into Turner's painting is happy for evermore.

But these metamorphoses are often alarming, sometimes cruel ('The Magic Morning', 'The River God'), sometimes doubtful: Muriel, like Scorpion, is still waiting for Death to take her out; the frog prince has mixed feelings about becoming a 'disenchanted' prince and giving up the 'quiet life' of a frog. One of her more childish poems has the epigram 'This is not kind', and she says of poetry that, like a classical deity, 'she is very strong and never has any kindness at all'. False, cosy enchantments are dangerous, like the fairy-tale of Christianity. Trusting innocents have to be educated into disenchantment and experience, like the children in 'At School', or the little boy who has to learn how to write a business letter (p. 103). Innocent childish characters may be 'translated' into another existence (Arthur in 'The Blue from Heaven') or else hung from the gallows ('One of Many') but if innocence is to survive in the real world it must compromise. The poems are full of fierce, lonely misfits who choose not to join in

('Croft', 'My Heart was Full', 'Scorpion', 'The Hostage', 'Magna est Veritas'): they prefer to play simple, as Stevie Smith's poetry does in part. These characters are waiting to be taken away: 'For it was not in this world that the Christians were desirous of being either useful or desirable' she once quoted from Gibbon in a poetry reading. They are passing through this world on the way to something better.

From the eight-year-old infant Pompey in *Novel on Yellow Paper* who makes up her mind that 'Death has got to come if I call him', to the aging Scorpion, who 'so wishes to be gone', Stevie Smith's versions of herself all take the Senecan attitude to suicide, as a noble and encouraging possibility, should life become 'more than I choose to bear'. Many of her poems summon Death as a friend and servant. (Her reaction to Virginia Woolf's suicide is tellingly matter-of-fact: 'just generally fed up all round I suppose' (*Me Again*, p. 277). But Stevie Smith did not kill herself (she once tried to), nor was she a recluse. Though she admires the simpletons like Croft, she is scornful of characters who give up altogether or fail for lack of courage ('The Deserter', 'The Weak Monk', 'The Recluse', 'The Failed Spirit'). The concomitant of the Senecan attitude to death is a stoicism about life (as in 'Ceux qui luttent . . .' and 'Away, Melancholy'). People who 'manage to keep going' under pressure or in pain are to be 'honoured and magnified', even if the pretence of being 'jolly and ordinary' and of 'feeling at home in the world' (phrases used during a poetry reading) sometimes breaks down, as in 'Not Waving but Drowning'. Even so, you must

> Smile, smile, and get some work to do
> Then you will be practically unconscious without positively
>   having to go.   (p. 153)

To do any more than that is to be a hero, like Harold, even if the heroic act turns out to be futile:

> I would not say that he was wrong,
> Although he succeeded in doing nothing but die.
>   (p. 111)

The argument in 'A Dream of Comparison' between Mary, who loves life ('I would fight to the death for it') and Eve, who longs for consciousness to cease ('Storm back through the gates of Birth') is central to all Stevie Smith's work.

'These are all very moral poems, you know (*Me Again*, p. 345). Under cover of playing simple or looking silly (as in 'Croft') she gives us firm opinions about behaviour. In some of the more didactic poems, like those about cruelty to animals, a nagging tone can creep in:

> Of all the disgraceful and abominable things
> Making animals perform for the amusement of human
>   beings is
> Utterly disgraceful and abominable.

But indignation is an essential part of her writing: she is trenchant, belligerent, acidulous, argumentative, believing with Blake that anger teaches sense (p. 133). Her most passionate quarrel is with the Church: she distrusts Christianity's 'sweetness and cruelty', and its system of prizes and punishments, she has a horror of religious persecution and fanaticism (see the deceptively comical 'Our Bog is Dood' and 'The House of Over-Dew'), a wry distaste for Jesuitical wiles, and an impatience with the modern Church's vulgar attempts to talk down and to popularize. (There is a furious poem about the alterations to the Prayer Book, and a furious review of the New English Bible in *Me Again*.) Though she writes some stirring poems of belief ('God the Eater', 'The Airy Christ') her more characteristic treatment of religion is in her fine anguished poems of debate ('Was He Married?' 'Thoughts about the Christian Doctrine of Eternal Hell', 'How Do You See?').

Stevie Smith is a fierce critic of male privileges. Living her whole life in 'a house of female habitation'—*Novel on Yellow Paper* tells the story of 'daddy's' disappearance and of the Aunt's adoption of Pompey and her sister after their mother's death—she is caustic about the common forms of male chauvinism. Tyrannical husbands like Major Macroo or the 'tigers' of 'Bottle Green' (p. 64), bossy male bureaucrats and smug male writers get short shrift. Sex is fun (cenobites are as bad as dictators) but the boyfriends in the novels are always a bore in the end, and girls who can't say no are urged to be more fierce and proud. Domestic bliss (closely observed on visits to married couples) is outweighed by the pleasures of female friendship and of a gregarious independence, worth the risk of loneliness. And she writes as savagely about the cruelty *of* children as about cruelty *to* them.

Her idiosyncratic feminism is only one element in her social and political satire. Here the relationship between prose and poetry is very close: 'Who Shot Eugenie?' (p. 123) is a version of *Over the Frontier*; the poetic treatment of war ('The Lads of the Village', 'Private Means is Dead'), of the upper classes ('A Father for a Fool') and of the literary establishment ('Tom Snooks the Pundit') is reworked in the fictions; and many of the political poems are put into the novels as part of the long debates on war, empire, government, power, and English society.

Her political attitudes might best be described by comparing her with the great Victorian reformist writers. Carlyle's *Sartor Resartus* and Arnold's *Culture and Anarchy* loom behind her savage moral irritation with English complacency and vulgarity, and the vigorous authority with which she defines the English virtues (p. 104). She has a passion for English places —Lincolnshire, the Humber, Norfolk, the sea at Swanage, the North London suburb where she lived from the age of three, the Home Counties: 'I suspect that for me Hertfordshire is the operative word' (*Over the Frontier*, p. 33). She detests what she considers to be English decadence and preciousness—Pater, the Pre-Raphaelites, the Bloomsbury group, Anglo-Catholicism, upper-class inbreeding, homosexuals—as much as she dislikes the middle-class snobbery of the suburbs and the commercial vulgarity of the 'women's' magazines published by the firm she worked for, Newnes and Pearson. All this Old English Toryism is best summed up by her devotion to her Dickensian aunt, with whom she lived in Palmers Green, and whose crabby eccentricities earned her the same nickname as the British Empire's, the 'lion'.

But though opinionated and intolerant, her arguments against tyranny and stupidity are not simplistic. Her painful quarrel with Christianity is symptomatic of how much she is torn and divided. She loves Germany, but sees early in the 1930s to what it is moving. She hates anti-Semitism, but knows what it can feel like, and that a single thought of it can 'swell the mass of cruelty working up against them' (*Novel on Yellow Paper*, p. 107). She defends the Empire, but knows that nothing becomes it like the relinquishing of its conquests (as in India). She has no patience with pacifism in the face of the Nazis, but knows that war brings out the darkness in people. In overthrowing cruelty one can become cruel. When Pompey puts on a uniform in *Over the*

Frontier she finds barbarism, military ambition, and the fanaticism of a nationalist ideology latent in herself.

Stevie Smith's political thoughts are realist and anti-romantic. It is not revolutions which stir her, but 'the time when revolutions succeed and must govern', and the pragmatic question of compromise is raised: 'Can resistance pass to government and not take to itself the violence of its oppressors, the absolutism and the torture?' (*The Holiday*, p. 9). There must, she supposes, always be 'a loss, a falling off, a distortion', in politics as in Christianity, when 'thought passes into word, idea into action, revolution into government' (*Me Again*, p. 168). Nevertheless, for all her satire and grief, she is a meliorist, in the tradition of Victorian writers such as Tennyson and Carlyle. It is 'touch and go', but there are signs that man may be coming out of the mountains. At least 'Man aspires/To good', at least we may be approaching a time when men 'love love and hate hate but do not deify them'. One must be disenchanted, but hopeful:

> Away, melancholy,
> Away with it, let it go.

Hermione Lee

Stevie Smith: Biography and Bibliography

———————————— * ————————————

Born Florence Margaret Smith, 20 September 1902, in Hull.

Moved to Palmers Green (1 Avondale Road) in 1905.

Educated at Palmers Green High School and North London Collegiate School for Girls.

Worked as secretary and personal assistant for the magazine publishers Sir George Newnes and Sir Neville Pearson from the 1920s to the 1950s.

Awarded the Cholmondeley Award for Poetry and, in 1969, the Queen's Gold Medal for poetry.

Died 7 March 1971.

FICTION

Novel on Yellow Paper (Cape, 1936; Virago, 1980)

Over the Frontier (Cape, 1938; Virago, 1980)

The Holiday (Chapman and Hall, 1949; Virago, 1979)

POETRY

A Good Time Was Had By All (Cape, 1937)

Tender Only To One (Cape, 1938)

Mother, What Is Man? (Cape, 1942)

Harold's Leap (Cape, 1950)

Not Waving but Drowning (Deutsch, 1957)

Some Are More Human Than Others: A Sketch-Book (Gabberbocchus, 1958)

Selected Poems (Longmans, 1962): includes 17 previously uncollected poems

The Frog Prince (Longmans, 1966): includes 69 previously uncollected poems

Two In One (Longmans, 1971): reprint of *Selected Poems* (1962) and *The Frog Prince*

Scorpion and Other Poems (Longmans, 1972): Introduction by Patric Dickinson

Collected Poems (Allen Lane, 1975): Introduction by James MacGibbon

Selected Poems, ed. James MacGibbon, (Penguin, 1978)

EDITIONS

Cats in Colour (Batsford, 1959)

Batsford Book of Children's Verse, ed. Elizabeth Jennings (Batsford, 1958); reissued as *Favourite Verse* (Chancellor Press, 1970) 1970)

COLLECTIONS

Me Again: Uncollected Writings of Stevie Smith, ed. Jack Barbera and William McBrien (Virago, 1981): Preface by James MacGibbon

ESSAYS ON STEVIE SMITH

'Talking to Stevie' and 'Thinking about Stevie', in Kay Dick, *Ivy and Stevie* (Duckworth, 1971)

'Did Nobody Teach You?' (1971), in D. J. Enright, *Man is an Onion: Reviews and Essays* (Chatto and Windus, 1972)

'Stevie Smith', in Calvin Bedient, *Eight Contemporary Poets* (Oxford University Press, 1974)

'A Memorable Voice' (1976), in Seamus Heaney, *Preoccupations* (Faber and Faber, 1980)

'Stevie Smith' by Christopher Ricks in *Grand Street*, Autumn 1981, Vol. I, no. 1, pp. 147–157

'Stevie, Good-bye' by Philip Larkin in the *Observer*, 23 January 1972

SELECTIONS IN

The Faber Book of Twentieth Century Verse, ed. John Heath-Stubbs (1953)

Penguin Modern Verse Selection (with Edwin Brock and Geoffrey Hill) (1966)

The Oxford Book of Twentieth Century Verse, ed. Philip Larkin (1973)

The Oxford Book of Contemporary Verse, ed. D. J. Enright (1980)

Novel on Yellow Paper (1936)

———————— * ————————

'A foot-off-the-ground novel'

But first, Reader, I will give you a word of warning. This is a foot-off-the-ground novel that came by the left hand. And the thoughts come and go and sometimes they do not quite come and I do not pursue them to embarrass them with formality to pursue them into a harsh captivity. And if you are a foot-off-the-ground person I make no bones to say that is how you will write and only how you will write. And if you are a foot-on-the-ground person, this book will be for you a desert of weariness and exasperation. So put it down. Leave it alone. It was a mistake you made to get this book. You could not know.

And it is not to be proud I say: I am a foot-off-the-ground person; or to be superior that I say: Foot-on-the-ground person —Keep out. It is to save you an exasperation and weariness that have now already hardly brought you to this early page.

But if you do not know whether you are a foot-off-the-ground person or a foot-on-the-ground person, then I say, Come on. Come on with me, and find out.

And for my part I will try to punctuate this book to make it easy for you to read, and to break it up, with spaces for a pause, as the publisher has asked me to do. But this I find very extremely difficult.

For this book is the talking voice that runs on, and the thoughts come, the way I said, and the people come too, and come and go, to illustrate the thoughts, to point the moral, to adorn the tale.

Oh talking voice that is so sweet, how hold you alive in captivity, how point you with commas, semi-colons, dashes, pauses and paragraphs?

Foot-on-the-ground person will have his grave grave doubts, and if he is also a smug-pug he will not keep his doubts to himself; he will say: It is not, and it cannot come to good. And I shall say,

Yes it is and shall. And he will say: So you think you can do this, so you do, do you?

Yes I do, I do.

That is my final word to smug-pug. You all now have been warned.

'Those Victorian days'

How richly compostly loamishly sad were those Victorian days, with a sadness not nerve-irritating like we have today. How I love those damp Victorian troubles. The woods decay, the woods decay and fall, The vapours weep their burthen to the ground, Man comes and tills the field and lies beneath, And after many a summer dies the swan. Yes, always someone dies, someone weeps, in tune with the laurels dripping, and the tap dripping, and the spout dripping into the water-butt, and the dim gas flickering greenly in the damp conservatory.

And the laurels so teeming and close along the drive, a human foot was bound to feel there was something behind it all. *Behind the laurel bushes lay the corpse of Sir Vyvyan Markaby, Baronet.*

Then I think of the wild wet days of the wild wet Lincolnshire of the younger Tennyson. How, were there two? Yes, but I mean younger than the pet of the Old Queen. Younger and sadder. Oh the sad sweet over-sweet Alfred, so haughty, so proud and so disagreeable.

And thinking of all this I have a great *nostalgie* for an open drain, like the flooded dykes they have there between the sodden fields.

'The German people'

. . . that Eckhardt neurosis got more and more pronounced. Always Trudi was having her hands smacked at meals for putting them on the table, and then she had to be told a fairy story, and all the time it was just the one fairy story that I got nearly by heart. Reader, it was The Wolf and the Seven Little Kids, and when it ended up *Der Wolf ist tot, Der Wolf ist tot.* Hurra, hurra, hurra, the blood lust and ferocity on the infant face of the infant neurotic was something more than I could stand.

And there was another one she would allow sometimes to be told. It is the one about Snowdrop and her cruel stepmother that was so vain she must be always looking in her wonder-mirror to say: *Spieglein, Spieglein an der Wand, Wer ist die schönste im ganzen Land?* But when the little Snowdrop was grown up, the mirror must tell the truth, so it must say in answer to the Queen's question: *Frau Königin, Ihr seid die schönste hier aber Schneewittchen ist tausendmal schöner als Ihr.* So this puts the Queen in a fine fume of rage and envy. So eventually Snowdrop is cast off into the forest, with all the other little German fairystory princesses. And by and by of course the little Snowdrop grows right up and marries her prince. And the wicked stepmother? Ah well, this is what happens to her. She falls in with the happy wedding-party and they take her by force and make her dance in red-hot shoes until she is dead: *Da musste sie in die rotglühenden Schuhe treten und so lange tanzen, bis sie tot zur Erde fiel.* See the idea? Well, try it on the baby.

Oh how deeply neurotic the German people is, oh how it goes right through and isn't just the leaders, like they pretend in *The Times*. Oh they are so strained and stretched and all the time they are wanting something so yearningly, it is something they don't quite know, like a dream or something that is out of focus. Oh they are wanting it all the time and stretching out their hands, oh you feel you must cover your face, it is not decent to look at that.

It is like that Sir Phoebus that is back in Rule Britannia, with his dark face and capacity for getting bored, like he gets more bored more quickly than anyone I know, like he said about his fountain pen, that day it squirted up all over his face, and the next day it did the same, only it squirted all over my frock, and he said: Why the old pen is getting vicious in its old age, it's getting real vice into it, we shall have it peeping through a keyhole soon, peeping through the keyhole at a franc a time. See.

Well I had that feeling in Germany, like the people were stripping themselves too naked, and doing it with oh such lovey-dovey yearning, yes, and saying: Is there anything more beautiful than the naked body? Oh yes thanks, right off without any call to hard work, I can think of things that are a whole lot more beautiful than the naked body.

Well this nakedness of Germany, with all its whimpering lovey dovey get-all-together, and with its Movements, and Back to Wotan, and Youth Youth Youth, it makes you feel: God send the British Admiralty and the War Office don't go shuffling on with their arms economies too long-o.

Ugh that hateful feeling I had over there, and how it was a whole race was gone run mad. Oh heaven help Deutschland when it kicks out the Jews, with their practical intelligence that might keep Germany from all that dream darkness, like the forests had got hold of them again, and the Romans calling their Legions back along the Via Aurelia.

'The Bacchae'

Now the story of *Phèdre* is very well known, but perhaps the story of the *Bacchae* is not so well known. But it is a story that I shall now tell you, and you will think it is not very suitable for children. And no perhaps it is not very suitable for children, if you have that point of view about children. But this is a far better play than *Medea*, so now I will tell you.

It is about Dionysus, and there is a lot of Dionysus-magic in this play, that is a little bit frightening perhaps. Dionysus has no good feelings, no not one, he has no good feelings and no high sentiment, he is very cynical and laughs a lot, very cruel and very cynical. So he is the son of Zeus and Semele. And Pentheus is ruler of this Theban land. And Pentheus is the nephew of Semele that died, that was burnt up in a great flame, that died, and had her grave with the sacred fire burning on it always, that died, and Dionysus lived, and was taken by Zeus and held by Zeus in his thigh, till Dionysus was old enough to go about by himself.

So now Pentheus is living in the royal palace, and he has there with him his mother Agave, and other women of the Court. And no, Pentheus is very stubborn, rather stupid very stubborn. No, he will not recognize the divinity of Dionysus. He had played with Semele as a child. No, Semele never had a divine son. No aunt ever had a divine son, so he would not worship Dionysus. But the women and Agave they had feelings of forebodings about this sturdy attitude of Pentheus, they thought no good would come of it.

So presently Dionysus heard, and laughed and laughed, and came down to Thebes laughing and swift, and very divine and furious. And he was disguised. And he now drove the women mad, they were all driven mad, they ran to the mountains with the divine frenzy of madness upon them, and they ran and ran, leaving their husbands and their children. Up on the wild mountains they ran, and they had their thyrses, and there they were run mad on the wild mountains worshipping Dionysus, and so strong in their madness they would pick up wolf cubs, and hold them up and give them the milk that their children should have had, and they would laugh and laugh and hunt the lion, and capture him, and with their naked hands pull him to pieces, tear him, tear his head off, pull him entirely to pieces, they were so mad and so powerful in their madness. There were no women left in Thebes at all.

Now very softly and quietly, very deceitfully in the hot afternoon, Dionysus comes into the palace, the palace is very quiet and empty, he comes into the palace, nobody challenges him, he is laughing softly all the time. So he comes to the King, and he tells the King: Why is it Pentheus, where are all the women? But Dionysus is disguised, and the King is so sad because the women are all run mad, he does not think: I am a King, why should this curious-looking man question me? There is something about him I do not like. I do not trust him. Why should this man question me?

No, he talks with Dionysus always disguised, and laughing very softly to himself: Why Pentheus do you not follow the women and bring them back? Why *Pentheus*, the strong plain blunt straightforward man, so honest, with no nonsense, why nobody could get round you? Why, surely, surely you will follow the women, and bring them back? Why, it would be funny if you did anything else but follow the women and bring them back. Why, people would certainly laugh. Why, if I said: Why, Pentheus will not follow the women, he will let them go, he will let them go run mad. Why, at first they would not believe me. But we know Pentheus he is just a plain honest man, he is not that sort of man, it must be somebody else. But then so later they would believe me, and then they would believe me, and they would laugh, and presently the laughter would be very loud, and it would be very loud and it would last a very long time. And you would go into your palace. But no, the laughter would be there too, very loud, very clear. So you would go into your bedchamber, but at once you would see that it was impossible to go into your bedchamber, at once you would see that the bedchamber was full of the laughter, that it was there that the laughter was all the time: Well here it is, how foolish, and not outside at all as I thought.

So now Dionysus began to laugh out loud. At first he began to laugh very softly out loud, but then not so softly, and then very loudly, and then Pentheus began to laugh too: 'Why did I distrust this man?' He thinks: 'He is very funny, he has made me laugh, so now it is weeks since I have laughed.'

So later they are getting on finely together. And then Dionysus learns that Pentheus is afraid to go near the women, because they are god-driven-mad, and can tear lions apart, and will allow no man to go near them. No man is to go on that mountain, they will tear him apart like a lion.

So Dionysus says very softly, very winning and casual: But Pentheus my dear fellow, that's easy, dress up as a woman. Now there is something dishonourable for a King to dress up as a woman, but there is something no longer honourable at all in Pentheus, he is sniggering and laughing all the time, he no longer has any dignity, or any honour. So this is a fine idea his new friend had. So they laugh and laugh, and get women's clothes, and Dionysus drapes them round Pentheus: *My dear*, how do you like this peplum, do you think it goes? This fold looks better hanging so; don't you think? He makes the King turn and walk and turn, he is very difficult to satisfy is Dionysus. But at last every fold is in place, and the head gear is just right, and he gives him the thyrsis: My dear chap you look just like a rather serious-minded slightly pompous female, just like my old aunt I'll tell you about next time. My dear, nobody would think you weren't at least a woman, and perhaps an aunt and mother. Oh I think we'll let you keep your own sandals. *It's a pretty stiff climb up those mountains.*

So now Pentheus feels a little cold, as if he were caught in a swift current. So now he is beginning to feel he has to go up to that mountain and see those women, but it is a force coming from outside makes him have to, have to go.

So now Dionysus takes him by the arm, propelling him, very friendly very strong. Dionysus leads him, pushes him outside of the palace, and the current is getting swifter, and Pentheus doesn't even care so much about it now, he will just go, it doesn't matter much, his nice friend says to go, he's a jolly good fellow this friend, with heaps of funny ideas. So Pentheus goes along laughing, and laughing goes along out of the town, and up the path, getting narrower and steeper, and laughing softly to himself. And at the bend going out of sight he thinks he ought to have looked behind before, it's a bit ungrateful, with this nice friend of his helping him with all those funny ideas, it doesn't look a generous act at all to go straight on like he was, without ever turning to wave to that nice new friend of his. So he gets to the bend and looks down.

There is Dionysus looking taller and bigger, and different. And laughing. Like it wasn't so much a laugh, as something he can't put a name to, not so much a laugh, but it is a laugh, but a grin, something like he'd seen before, with all those teeth. Ha ha, he was just pulling a funny face, that was all, he certainly was a boy with funny ideas, it was nothing at all of course about his being bigger, it was just a trick of the distance. So: Good-bye, shouts Pentheus: Good-bye, and thanks a lot. And: Good-bye, shouts Dionysus: Good-bye Pentheus, give my love to Agave.

And Pentheus is never seen again alive.

This play that we did at school, with the professor I was saying about there himself, very approving and following on the script, made a very great impression on me, and I used to watch the scene in the palace where Dionysus is dressing up the King in women's clothes, and I used to laugh too, and laugh, and I used to think: Dionysus is wonderful.

'The Church'

But now I think the Church should stand up, should get right up now, and say: Stupidity is a sin. And then it should teach in very difficult to understand, very high-up language, not simple at all, but really very difficult, and it should teach the philosophy of Christianity in very high-up terms, and it should always speak high-up and well above people's heads, so they have trouble to understand. And then the church might be empty. Very good, let it be empty. But by and by people would get sick at the way they missed the point, and they would get on their mettle, and be clever. Well think, the clever way they do the crossword puzzles, like the clever way they grapple with Torquemada, and the intricacies of the Stock Exchange, and the intricacies of, well say the intricacies of the law of libel, which certainly is not easy to get the hang of, and the intricacies of, well say the intricacies of Somerset House, and the problems of taxation and economics. Well think now how many people in their separate way grapple with these difficult problems, which are departments of the mind, which are the same departments of the mind that would be called in to grapple with the problems of Christian apologetics. And was St Paul simply having Sunday evening chats not-a-bit-clever? Not he. He certainly was a clever one, was St Paul, very profound and cunning.

Well let the Church think it is in a non-Christian land, where the people are bone lazy about using their brains, but good enough at it if they're interested, and not only materially interested either, but knowing in a dim dark way sometimes that, but knowing that, only in using their minds to the utmost, and more, will they escape the fiend's heart of boredom. And let the Church go round and about, being very high-up in their preaching very deep and don't care, very; Don't-care-if-it-is-above-you, stretch-a-bit-you-lazy-hound. And not a bit affable and simple, and not very kind, but very deep and ingenious. Well look then they might try this. It certainly would be a change.

'A visitor'

I have travelled and come and gone a great deal, I am a *toute entière* visitor. That is what I am being all the time. I visit and visit and visit, my darling friends, my less darling friends, my acquaintances. I am very grateful to them all. In visiting I find a very great deal of comfort and satisfaction, and each least place where I visit I am so enchanted and so happy that it is another visit, and that at the end of the time I may say: Good-bye and thank you, good-bye. And perhaps as I have said they will stand and smile, and say: Good-bye Pompey, come again soon. That is the very highest pleasure to me, that it is a visit that comes to an end, that may recur, that may again come to an end and be renewed. The rhythm of visiting is in my blood. Under what tutelary deity shall I place myself? Under Mercury, double-facing, looking two ways, lord of the underworld, riding on the white horse, riding through hell, opener of doors; Hermes.

A Good Time Was Had By All (1937)

———————————— * ————————————

Alfred the Great

Honour and magnify this man of men
Who keeps a wife and seven children on £2 10
Paid weekly in an envelope
And yet he never has abandoned hope.

Egocentric

What care I if good God be
If he be not good to me,
If he will not hear my cry
Nor heed my melancholy midnight sigh?
What care I if he created Lamb,
And golden Lion, and mud-delighting Clam,
And Tiger stepping out on padded toe,
And the fecund earth the Blindworms know?
He made the Sun, the Moon and every Star,
He made the infant Owl and the Baboon,

He made the ruby-orbed Pelican,
He made all silent inhumanity,
Nescient and quiescent to his will,
Unquickened by the questing conscious flame
That is my glory and my bitter bane.
What care I if Skies are blue,
If God created Gnat and Gnu,
What care I if good God be
If he be not good to me?

Mrs Simpkins

Mrs Simpkins never had very much to do
So it occurred to her one day that the Trinity wasn't true
Or at least but a garbled version of the truth
And that things had moved very far since the days of her
    youth.
So she became a spiritualist and at her very first party
Just to give her a feeling of confidence the spirit spoke up
    hearty:
'Since I crossed over dear friends' it said 'I'm no different to
    what I was before
Death's not a separation or alteration or parting it's just a
    one-handled door
We spirits can come back to you if your seance is orthodox
But you can't come over to us till your body's shut in a box
And this is the great thought I want to leave with you today
You've heard it before but in case you forgot death isn't a
    passing away
It's just a carrying on with friends relations and brightness
Only you don't have to bother with sickness and there's no
    financial tightness.'
Mrs Simpkins went home and told her husband he was a weak
    pated fellow

And when he heard the news he turned a daffodil shade of
    yellow
'What do you mean, Maria?' he cried, 'it can't be true there's
    no rest
From one's uncles and brothers and sisters nor even the wife of
    one's breast?'
'It's the truth,' Mrs Simpkins affirmed, 'there is no separation
There's a great reunion coming for which this life's but a
    preparation.'
This worked him to such a pitch that he shot himself through
    the head
And now she has to polish the floors of Westminster County
    Hall for her daily bread.

To the Tune of
the Coventry Carol

The nearly right
And yet not quite
In love is wholly evil
And every heart
That loves in part
Is mortgaged to the devil.

I loved or thought
I loved in sort
Was this to love akin
To take the best
And leave the rest
And let the devil in?

O lovers true
And others too
Whose best is only better
Take my advice
Shun compromise
Forget him and forget her.

Night-Time in the Cemetery

The funeral paths are hung with snow
About the graves the mourners go
To think of those who lie below.
The churchyard pales are black against the night
And snow hung here seems doubly white.
I have a horror of this place
A horror of each moonlit mourner's face
These people are not familiar
But strange and stranger than strange peculiar
They have that look of a cheese do you know sour-sweet
You can smell their feet.
Yet must I tread
About my dead
And guess the forms within the grave
And hear the clank of jowl on jowl
Where low lies kin no love could save.
Yet stand I by my grave as they by theirs. Oh bitter Death
That brought their love and mine unto a coffin's breadth.

Infant

It was a cynical babe
Lay in its mother's arms
Born two months too soon
After many alarms
Why is its mother sad
Weeping without a friend
Where is its father—say?
He tarries in Ostend.
It was a cynical babe. Reader before you condemn, pause,
It was a cynical babe. Not without cause.

God and the Devil

God and the Devil
Were talking one day
Ages and ages of years ago.
God said: Suppose
Things were fashioned this way,
Well then, so and so.
The Devil said: No,
Prove it if you can.
So God created Man
And that is how it all began.
It has continued now for many a year
And sometimes it seems more than we can bear.
But why should bowels yearn and cheeks grow pale?
We're here to point a moral and adorn a tale.

From the County Lunatic Asylum

The people say that spiritism is a joke and a swizz,
The Church that it is dangerous—not half it is.

The Bereaved Swan

Wan
Swan
On the lake
Like a cake
Of soap
Why is the swan
Wan
On the lake?
He has abandoned hope.

Wan
Swan
On the lake afloat
Bows his head:
O would that I were dead
For her sake that lies
Wrapped from my eyes
In a mantle of death,
The swan saith.

Correspondence between Mr Harrison in Newcastle and Mr Sholto Peach Harrison in Hull

Sholto Peach Harrison you are no son of mine
And do you think I bred you up to cross the River Tyne
And do you think I bred you up (and mother says the same)
And do you think I bred you up to live a life of shame
To live a life of shame my boy as you are thinking to
Down south in Kingston-upon-Hull a traveller in glue?
Come back my bonny boy nor break your father's heart
Come back and marry Lady Susan Smart
She has a mint in Anglo-Persian oil
And Sholto never more need think of toil.

You are an old and evil man my father
I tell you frankly Sholto had much rather
Travel in glue unrecompensed unwed
Than go to church with oily Sue and afterwards to bed.

Aubade

My dove, my doe,
I love you so,
I cannot will not
Let you go,
'Tis not the day lights yonder sky
It is too soon
I hear the cock's discordant cry,
He doodles to the moon.
It is not day
I say
It is the moon.

Alas, my love, it is the day,
Born twin to sun, but opening first
The womb of night.
There lies the day,
Her cheeks are gray,
Alas so soon it is the day.
And now in agony her dam will try
To bring forth sun, and in fulfilment die.
No easy birth is here,
Before our eyes
Night bleeds
And, born caesareanwise,
Her son in flaming gear
Comes forth and her succeeds.
Once more for man the heavenly twins are born,
Farewell, my love, adieu, it is the dawn.

The River Deben

All the waters of the river Deben
Go over my head to the last wave even
Such a death were sweet to seven times seven.

Death sits in the boat with me
His face is shrouded but he smiles I see
The time is not yet, he will not come so readily.

But he smiles and I smile it is pleasant in the boat at night
There is no moon rising but from the east a light
Shines in the sky, is it dawn or dawn's twilight?

Over here the waters are dark as a deep chasm
Shadowed by cliffs of volcanic spasm
So dark so dark is the waves' fashion.

But the oars dip I am rowing they dip and scatter
The phosphorescence in a sudden spatter
Of light that is more actual than a piece of matter.

Up the Deben we row I row towards Waldringfield
It is a long way yet, my arms ache but will not yield
In this physical tiredness there is a happy shield.

Oh happy Deben, oh happy night, and night's companion Death,
What exultation what ecstasy is in thy breath
It is as salt as the salt silt that lies beneath.

Flow tidal river flow, draw wind from the east,
Smile pleasant Death, smile Death in darkness blessed,
But tarry day upon the crack of dawn. Thou comest unwished.

Little Boy Lost

The wood was rather old and dark
The witch was very ugly
And if it hadn't been for father
Walking there so smugly
I never should have followed
The beckoning of her finger.
Ah me how long ago it was
And still I linger
Under the ever interlacing beeches
Over a carpet of moss
I lift my hand but it never reaches
To where the breezes toss
The sun-kissed leaves above.
The sun?
Beware.
The sun never comes here.
Round about and round I go
Up and down and to and fro
The woodlouse hops upon the tree
Or should do but I really cannot see.
Happy fellow. Why can't I be
Happy as he?
The wood grows darker every day
It's not a bad place in a way
But I lost the way
Last Tuesday
Did I love father, mother, home?
Not very much; but now they're gone
I think of them with kindly toleration
Bred inevitably of separation.
Really if I could find some food
I should be happy enough in this wood
But darker days and hungrier I must spend
Till hunger and darkness make an end.

Bag-Snatching in Dublin

Sisley
Walked so nicely
With footsteps so discreet
To see her pass
You'd never guess
She walked upon the street.

Down where the Liffey waters' turgid flood
Churns up to greet the ocean-driven mud,
A bruiser in a fix
Murdered her for 6/6.

This Englishwoman

This Englishwoman is so refined
She has no bosom and no behind.

Major Macroo

Major Hawkaby Cole Macroo
Chose
Very wisely
A patient Griselda of a wife with a heart of gold
That never beat for a soul but him
Himself and his slightest whim.

He left her alone for months at a time
When he had to have a change
Just had to
And his pension wouldn't stretch to a fare for two
And he didn't want it to.

And if she wept she was game and nobody knew it
And she stood at the edge of the tunnel and waved as his train
    went through it.

And because it was cheaper they lived abroad
And did he care if she might be unhappy or bored?
He did not.
He'd other things to think of—a lot.

He'd fads and he fed them fat,
And she could lump it and that was that.

He'd several boy friends
And she thought it was nice for him to have them,
And she loved him and felt that he needed her and waited
And waited and never became exasperated.

Even his room
Was dusted and kept the same,
And when friends came
They went into every room in the house but that one
Which Hawkaby wouldn't have shown.

Such men as these, such selfish cruel men
Hurting what most they love what most loves them,
Never make a mistake when it comes to choosing a woman
To cherish them and be neglected and not think it inhuman.

All Things Pass

All things pass
Love and mankind is grass.

Private Means is Dead

Private Means is dead
God rest his soul, officers and fellow-rankers said.

Captive Good, attending Captain Ill
Can tell us quite a lot about the Captain, if he will.

Major Portion
Is a disingenuous person
And as for Major Operation well I guess
We all know what his reputation is.

The crux and Colonel
Of the whole matter
(As you may read in the Journal
If it's not tattered)

Lies in the Generals Collapse Debility Panic and Uproar
Who are too old in any case to go to the War.

Beware the Man

Beware the man whose mouth is small
For he'll give nothing and take all.

Breughel

The ages blaspheme
The people are weak
As in a dream
They evilly speak.

Their words in a clatter
Of meaningless sound
Without form or matter
Echo around.

The people oh Lord
Are sinful and sad
Prenatally biassed
Grow worser born bad.

They sicken oh Lord
They have no strength in them
Oh rouse up my God
And against their will win them.

Must thy lambs to the slaughter
Deliverèd be
With each son and daughter
Irrevocably?

From tower and steeple
Ring out funeral bells
Oh Lord save thy people
They have no help else.

Over the Frontier (1938)

*

'Georg Grosz'

My mind was full of art and I had a nostalgie to be looking at these high-up and elevating canvases and there was especially the one that is called 'Haute École'.

Now this one I will tell you about. So. There is this very classical animal, this horse, that has a vivid plastique tail and his front leg is raised up to do the high step. His colour is a light and beautiful brown colour that hardly serves to cover the canvas, so ethereal and noble is this animal and his nostrils are spread wide. Very elegant indeed and high-born is this horse with his wide open eyes his wide-spread nostrils his sleek coat and his wide wide eyes that have that look in them that is a warning to the people that know about horses like me. But oh how splendid is this high and elegant horse that has in him and in his limpid and ferocious eye all the sense of that 'Hohe Schule' and all of the centuries of traditional comportment. On this horse's back sits a man that is perhaps not so entirely classique as this noble animal, because I am thinking now there is something about this man that is a little fin de siècle, for instance he is long and slim but though this is how the long lines of his body lie there is also at the same time about him that feeling of plumpness that is a little feminine and his face is so plump as the faces of some of the slim full faced pouting degenerate people that you have in the drawings of Beardsley. So. He has no hair on his head at all he is absolutely bald and his head has a pink plump covering of soft flesh and his lips are pursed and pouting and his eyes beneath puffed eyelids are looking downwards. Very sly very supercilious are the lineaments of this man's face. His long slim body is clad in black, it is a sort of 'smoking' he is wearing. He has no hat and there is no hat in the picture, so if he falls if he falls well shall I say that he will not fall a victim to a horrible whore, but if that malicious and indignant horse if he prances sideways and makes suddenly to shy then off will come the man, pitching forward on to the hard floor of the riding school and with nothing between his plump pink hairless head and the hard hard floor it will go hard with him I guess it will be all up with that hatless rider.

Oh the colour in this canvas how lovely it is how beautiful how lightly touched in with what skill and what wisdom so to leave the canvas bare with such precision with such significance to express so much to be so entirely necessary inevitable so never to be thought of until it is done and then how else could it ever have been thought of for one moment to be done.

Oh there is a very great genius in this picture and oh now how greatly I am wishing to possess it. So I say to the man who is in this elegant picture-gallery, he is a little short of breath, I ask him to tell me how much is this beautiful picture for which I have so great a tendre and this acquisitive feeling that possess it I must. Oh it is nothing says the short-of-breath man it is nothing just forty guineas that is what it is and is. O heart of pain and empty purse how come to forty guineas that is so much of what I have not got. So he says: *Very witty this painter is he not?* Oh yes, he certainly is the funny man. But oh I have a tendre for this horse and rider so I must look at the other pictures and forget and forget. I know this artist very well I know his black-and-white work, but never before have I seen his paintings and never before should I have thought for one moment that he could have projected this thought of this ferocious and captive animal and his degenerate rider. Oh hush now hush and remember to be reasonable and to look here and there, and to judge and to discriminate and not to make a fuss-up about this ha-ha horse that never can be yours. So. There are a lot of still lifes, no they are not anything so good, no I will say now that I am not partial to Mr Grosz's still lifes. Very often have they been painted by painters before to be hung in galleries, they are, this is what I should say, the still lifes of to-day in the current mood, that is to say there is that seashell Gefühl about them and the superficial incongruity of selection that is not contributing anything that is fresh but is only just superficially incongruous like I mean like a bad Bernard Shaw. So. But then there are some very cynical and malicious black-and-whites and colour-washes that take me right off again right off my heart of pride to say No he is not so good. But there is quickly now I will tell you there is 'The Assignation', that is certainly very funny: the girlie is rather fat and has on those funny 1928 clothes very short in the skirt and very high in the hat and so looking like a bolster that has short fat legs that go bulging over the cheap thin shoes. There is a sugar daddy that is looking at the girlie he is thinking he is thinking Well is she worth it, chaps, is she worth this famous RM 20 note that is at the present moment safe in my elegant pigskin pochette? And on the whole you guess the answer will be, I will knock her down to RM 10. I said I'll knock her down to RM 10. I said RM 10 is my limit. I said. There is also number 79 that is called 'Girl Guides' that I think will certainly not have at all a great appeal for Lady Baden-Powell. There are these girl guides, there are these two girls sitting on the ground and the curve of their plump thighs comes out of the too tight elastic band of their directoire knickers. So. One is playing a mouth-organ, very arch is the look in the eyes of this one, and the other sits and sings and sings with her mouth wide open and her little teeth, too small too small for the English taste, so very much too small too sharp and too white. There is something vicious about these sharp small white teeth that is offensive to the English taste that has always a fundamental but often unarticulated and even unrecognized preference for teeth that are long and strong and looking rather yellow. No. 77 is 'On the Beach'. This made me laugh and there I stood laughing and laughing, with the man who is perhaps only rather short of breath standing beside me. 'On the Beach' goes like this. There is a beachbasket like they have at Swinemünde and all along the flat coastline of the Ost-See bathing resorts. In this beachbasket is sitting an old girl who is really so extremely ugly and so extremely amorous that it is something to give you a good laugh. Three cheers for the old girl in the beachbasket that is peering round the corner of the beachbasket that is looking this way. She has a sharp pointed nose and little eager pig eyes and a hat raked on her head that has wisps of hay-hair rioting out from underneath this so-smart toque. And what is she looking at what is she looking at oh? Well, chaps, she is sitting looking at a fine nordic specimen that is full to the brim with masculine buck and that has such a cast in his eye that. Oh Strandkorb shield me from the strange man with the cast in his eye. But no, she must have her love and affection and also he is holding a camera. Oh scintillating vanity of unsatisfied desire, oh what a pity it is that the beach is so jam full of girls and boys and bathing attendants and ice-cream vendors that never for one moment can they be alone, oh certainly it is punk for those two that never can they be alone to obtain *eine seelische Entlassung* and a nice holiday snap to set on the mantelshelf beside the artificial roses. And looking and laughing and thinking of all this my thoughts turn again to a darker memorial I have of Georg Grosz that is this dark memorial that is called A Post-War Museum where all of the ignobility and shameful pain of war suffering is set down with the precision of genius and the bitterness of a complete experience, oh here in this portfolio are such things as our security cannot conceive, cannot bear for one moment to contemplate. People say, Why, such things cannot be true, no it is a neurosis, why this George Grosz he is just a war neurotic, it is sad but he should certainly be shut up and prevented, why it is not at all a good thing that he should be let run round to infect with his neurosis his defeatism his anti-sozialismus the healthy unthinking happiness of our sheltered infant adults.

But oh the tearing seering suffering of Germany after the war, the disintegration and diminution the backward journeying the fear the cringing corroding terror of poverty and hopelessness, The Old Men of 1922, the old broken shamefully broken body of the shattered soldier drawn up lifted up crucified upon his crutches lifted up above the old-young child, and over it all and undertoning it all is shame and loss and flight into darkness. Oh no no no, for us there is now not this Post-War Museum at all it is not in our experience we do not wish to understand or to think about it at all, it is for us somebody else's cup of tea that we do not even say: May it pass from us, that we do not have anything at all to do with. So a victory has given us at least this that we do not have to taste this cup of tea. No. For us there is this funny-ha-ha Georg Grosz that has his witty drawings and paintings in this elegant picture-gallery I was telling you. So Georg Grosz is out of Germany now he has made an escape to America and I am glad that he has done so. So now he can forget, or with the will not to remember he can have his American citizenship, and he can be still perhaps a little bitter and have his cynical laughter go echoing round the picture-galleries of London and New York, but it is only, Very funny, very clever, is it not? So he has created this laughing and ferocious horse, this so classical animal with his wide wide eyes that are so full of passion and integrity, oh this high-stepping horse that is so high up and arrogant, how very pure is his colouring how plastic and precise the draughts-manship this picture that is forty guineas, and what is there still to say about the rider? He is perhaps rather a nigger in the woodpile, there is perhaps something a little enigmatical about this rider, after all what is he doing? I think he is doing this, with great application and concentration this is what he is doing, he is forgetting to remember the shame and dishonour the power of the cruelty the high soaring flight of that earlier éclaircissement, that was that pale éclair dans une nuit profonde, that rakehell of a beam of light that went showing up the very sad bones of that earlier situation, this he is very actively forgetting and instead he will think of the easy generous light-running laughter of the English and Americans, and he is thinking of that American nationality that shall come dropping down dropping like a curtain to shut off from him for ever that sad sad situation, that already perhaps he is a little ashamed to have seen once and for all time so top to bottom, so round and about and within, so in its flesh and bones and skeleton its sinews nerves and muscles, to the very last outposts of the black heart of despair of the situation.

'Casmilus'

But once inside of the house of Hades, is there any outcoming? Oh yes, my chicks, for anyone of my name there is passage to and fro, come at will and go at pleasure. But enough of the Casmilus motif, shiftiest of namesakes, most treacherous lecherous and delinquent of Olympians, enough. The very name stinks to heaven, wrapped in whatever concealment of Phoenician Carthaginian double dealing. Avaunt. But always for Pluto I have this soft feeling of gentle pity and suffering. Despised and humiliated by Olympian lovelies, can you blame him if he ran off with the girl from Enna?

There was something sad about the boy, and sweet too, I dare say sweet enough, before he got set up with Minos and Rhadamanthus to judge the souls of all men. And in that gloomy residence, with my abominable namesake in his Punic or Grecian aspect coming uninvited, going unpermitted, conducting on the side a nefarious business to his own advantage, could the boy keep sweet? With what of irritation seething beneath the well bred and polite exterior of the enforced host? 'My dear Hermes-Cas, we are always delighted to see you, of course, there is no need for me to say that. But really sometimes you know (old friends are permitted to be frank) Persephone and I would appreciate a word in advance. At the moment for instance it is perhaps in the slightest way inconvenient. Only in this way my dear fellow, best of friends, most faithful of visitors, only in *this* way, that at this moment we are not able to devote to you the *attention*, to promote and arrange the *entertainment*, your versatility deserves.' Here Pluto would fetch a sigh. 'You see how it is, my hands are so full. The case list grows longer every day. Ah you travellers, you can never know how inimical to hospitality is the legal profession.'

'Never mind about me, dear boy,' says Cas, 'I can look after myself' (grim phrase productive of plutonic wince). 'There's a little business connected with Heracles. I'll blow in and see you again later.'

And off goes Cas leaving Pluto to grind his teeth and ponder again the strange uses of kingship, when even within his own realm, on this side of Styx and Phlegethon if you please, the brawling cantankerous buffoonish antics of the god and the hero are to be allowed free rein. Only in the sweet calm eyes of Persephone is there peace and consolation. Sighing again he turns into the Court House, sighing again to think that no rose is without thorn, and even Persephone must have a mother. The ebony portal clangs behind him. It will go hard with the dead to-day.

'Professor Dryasdust and Pater'

It was not long since that I was again in Edinburgh with my Aunt and at dinner with this young professor Dryasdust and his wife. Can the thirties mix with the twenties? I think it already begins to be a little difficult. How aggressive the boy is, how young and how cross. He has a great deal of book knowledge, and outside of books he knows nothing. He is a clever baby, will he ever be anything more, I do not know, in a moment of irritation I guess not. Already the rime of the pedant is upon his young bones. And his pugnacity, the aggressiveness of his prejudice, it is to be heard to be believed. But what has he to offer that one should put up with his abominable manner? Nothing but the derived heartiness of the Belloc and the Beachcomber and the oversimplification of life so dear to the rigid anglo-catholic intellectual. . . .

When I am walking with the wife of the professor Dryasdust we are getting along well enough. But when we turn back to dinner and he is there it is all very extremely painfully, not so good at all. Don't you dare to put Paracelsus in your book, he shouts at me, blue eyes hot in hot face. And why should I not put Paracelsus in my book, have you made a corner in Paracelsus, is Paracelsus now and forever to be your speciality, *spécialité de chez Dryasdust*? I won't have it, he screams. Then I shall put him in at once. I shout at him, he shouts at me, his wife falls sulky-silent, regarding the vegetable dishes, regarding the french beans fried in vinegar and butter by Bavarian cookie who is also rather cross and pounding in and out to shout cross Bavarian dialect at the English nuisances.

Ah this is a very painful situation now, and for once I am becoming I am really beginning to feel a little—well it is for instance embarrassing is it not. Girlie Dryasdust comes out of her vegetable reverie to say with biting precision to her husband something that is so bitingly precise it should not be said to husbands in front of helpless guest. How much money have you got in the Bank? Crescendo of anger and affront: We are living beyond our income. Oh return to the vegetable reverie dear Mrs Dryasdust, no alas never can the vegetable reverie if returned to be quite what it was before, so happy, so quiet, so inconspicuous, leaving to the professor and myself the onus of the quarrel. I am appalled, perhaps they are going to have a fight. I think now I am a little sorry for the sweet boy, I have no doubt at all that his wife is . . . well is she not? Oh peinliches Situation. I draw his fire again upon myself. Why for instance, I say, are you so furious with me, why are you this cross-dog that cannot speak for fury and whose countenance changes so often from the pale to the extremely red it is like Stratford Canning when the Turks in council with him begged him to control the choler that too faithfully drove the blood to his face for all to note? Is it perhaps because you wish yourself to write? Me? roars Dryasdust, I am writing a thesis on Paracelsus. Now by this time we are up from the table and sitting around. So Dryasdust takes down a volume of Pater and this is to show me that this indeed is prose that I could not have known. It is a pity I could not have known before, but you see it is a pity, but here is my chance here is my chance now to learn for the first time, if indeed it is not already too late. He sighs, takes his pipe from his mouth and reads. And reads. Oh but it is dreadful. Now this is what I cannot bear to support for one moment longer. The too-ripeness, the concealed verse forms, the succulent young voice of the insufferably teaching young professor, the falling back of the ten years since I read Pater, the too familiar and infuriating intrinsic cadences, the dying fall at the end of each paragraph. And the eyelids are a little weary . . . The return of the pagan world, the sins of the Borgias . . . And tinged the eyelids and the hands. Darling, I say, turning to his wife, I cannot support this. Pussy not feel well. I collect my hat, my gloves. I think of the most impossible unguestly things to say. I do not say them. Here the thirties are at a disadvantage. We think but cannot say. They say but cannot think. I think: Yes at twenty one may read Pater—but not aloud to friends, not that, never that, at twenty it is even commendable to read Pater, it shows that at least one has an ear for the less subtle harmonies of English prose. At twenty I could, but I hope did not, quote just that passage, but without the book. Here I am getting a little superior. In my moment of wicked crossness and superiority I think again of his essay on Paracelsus, and I think, but do not say: there is another quotation that will I think fit that very well, oh very well indeed. It is by a greater than Pater. And I think and I laugh and I think: To win the applause of schoolboys and furnish matter for a prize essay. Good-bye, now, I must go, I say. I have on my hat and gloves. I go, they come with me to my hotel. I glance at the clock. It is nine. So with all my forbearance the greatest insult is upon my side. It is 9 o'clock in the evening.

When I Awake

When I awake
The whole returning flood of consciousness
Is hateful to me
And Death, too often on my lips,
Becomes my shadower.

O Death, Death, Death, deceitful friend,
Come pounce, and take,
And make
An end at once.

'Married to a tiger'

Why do some women like to be bullied, I think to myself, lying at full length to enjoy the hot soft water. Now, at home where my aunt and I live, the wives are so often delighted to tell you how splendidly bullying their husbands are, and how they put the foot down here and there, and no, they will not let them play bridge in the afternoon and they will not let them smoke, 'My dear husband does not like to see me smoke', there is a great deal of pride in their voices when they say this, I have often noticed it, it is as if they would say, You may not think it but I am married to a tiger. No, I did not think it, for certainly I cannot penetrate this excellent disguise that this tiger has adopted, for certainly no better disguise for a tiger exists anywhere than the disguise of a Bottle Green husband. 'My dear,' say the jungle tiger-bucks, 'I shall go to the tiger reunion festival as a Bottle Green husband, you won't know me.'

'Power'

Is then power and the lust for power the very stuff of our existence, the prop of our survival, our hope of the future, our despair of the past? And if we cannot achieve in our individualities this power are we any less guilty if we pursue it, or again, abandoning the sweet chase, identify ourselves with a national ethos, take pride in our country, in our country's plundering, or, if the mood takes us, in our country's victories upon other fields less barren, in science, art, jurisprudence, philosophy? Ours the privilege, to us the laurels. Oh corruption, of uncertain mortality, how divide, without a national death, the springs of our being, brought forth in pain and set to its infliction? . . .

The thought and desire upon death is no salve for my mood, is but a cipher, an ignis fatuus, a foolish gesture, a child's scream of pain. Not self-violence upon the flesh, not a natural death, has promise of release. Power and cruelty are the strength of our life, and in its weakness only is there the sweetness of love.

Tender Only To One (1938)

————————— * —————————

Tender Only To One

Tender only to one
Tender and true
The petals swing
To my fingering
Is it you, or you, or you?

Tender only to one
I do not know his name
And the friends who fall
To the petals' call
May think my love to blame.

Tender only to one
This petal holds a clue
The face it shows
But too well knows
Who I am tender to.

Tender only to one,
Last petal's latest breath
Cries out aloud
From the icy shroud
His name, his name is Death.

O Happy Dogs of England

O happy dogs of England
Bark well as well you may
If you lived anywhere else
You would not be so gay.

O happy dogs of England
Bark well at errand boys
If you lived anywhere else
You would not be allowed to make such an infernal noise.

The Bishops of the Church of England

I admire the Bishops of the Church of England
No man can be a Bishop of the Church of England
And a fool.
A man can be a Bishop of the Church of England
And a knave.
But
Fortunately
Few if any of the Bishops of the Church of England
Are men of ill will.
They do their best
To resolve wisely
To govern effectively.
They are the butt of the ignoramus,
Of the sentimentalist,
Of the man who makes
Of his own bad temper and incompetency
A Movement for the Amelioration of the Sufferings
Of the Oppressed Members of the Lower Middle Classes.

One of Many

You are only one of many
And of small account if any,
You think about yourself too much.
This touched the child with a quick touch
And worked his mind to such a pitch
He threw his fellows in a ditch.
This little child
That was so mild
Is grown too wild.

Murder in the first degree, cried Old Fury,
Recording the verdict of the jury.

Now they are come to the execution tree.
The gallows stand wide. Ah me, ah me.

Christ died for sinners, intoned the Prison Chaplain from his
    miscellany.
Weeping bitterly the little child cries: I die one of many.

The Doctor

You are not looking at all well, my dear,
In fact you are looking most awfully queer.
Do you find that the pain is more than you can bear?

Yes, I find that it is more than I can bear, so give me some bromide
And then I will go away for a long time and hide
Somewhere on the seashore where the tide

Coming upon me when I am asleep shall cover
Me, go over entirely,
Carry beyond recovery.

Come, Death (i)

Why dost thou dally, Death, and tarry on the way?
When I have summoned thee with prayers and tears, why dost
    thou stay?
Come, Death, and carry now my soul away.

Wilt thou not come for calling, must I show
Force to constrain thy quick attention to my woe?
I have a hand upon thy Coat, and will
Not let thee go.

How foolish are the words of the old monks,
In Life remember Death.
Who would forget
Thou closer hangst on every finished breath?
How vain the work of Christianity
To teach humanity
Courage in its mortality.

Who would not rather die
And quiet lie
Beneath the sod
With or without a god?

Foolish illusion, what has Life to give?
Why should man more fear Death than fear to live?

Silence and Tears

A priestly garment, eminently suitable for conducting funeral services in
inclement weather.

From a church outfitter's catalogue

The tears of the widow of the military man
Fell down to the earth as the funeral sentence ran.
Dust to dust, Oh how frightful sighed the mourners as the rain
    began.

But the grave yawned wide and took the tears and the rain,
And the poor dead man was at last free from all his pain,
Pee-wee sang the little bird upon the tree again and again.

Is it not a solemn moment when the last word is said,
And wrapped in cloak of priestly custom we dispose our dead,
And the earth falls heavy, heavy, upon the expensive coffin lined
    with lead?

And may the coffin hold his bones in peace that lies below,
And may the widow woman's tears make a good show,
And may the suitable priestly garment not let the breath of
  scandal through.

For the weather of their happening has been a little inclement,
And would people be so sympathetic if they knew how the story
  went?
Best not put it to the test. Silence and tears are convenient.

A Father for a Fool

To the tune 'Boys and Girls Come out to Play'

Little Master Home-from-School,
This is the Parkland you must rule.
What does it feel like to have a father for a fool?
Your father mortgaged the estate,
Lost his money, blamed fate
And shot himself through the head too late.
There's a father for a fool,
My little Master Home-from-School.

Why does Auntie wear such funny hats
And invert her sentences? Now that's
Positive proof she must be bats.
Why has Parker got all the horses out for me?
Why doesn't Ma meet the train as usually?
Here's hoping they give us shrimps for tea.

Little Master Home-from-School,
Your Ma lies dead, she lies too cool,
She's stone cold dead of a broken heart, the fool.
Jingle-jog the horses go,
And Parker's thinking what I know:
Here comes Master Home-from-School
That had a father for a fool.

To a Dead Vole

Now Vole art dead
And done is all thy bleeding.
Thy soul is sped
And all thy body's heeding
For daily bread
And comfortable bed
Has brought thee where there's no more thought of feeding,
And where the soil is thy last unappreciated quilt.

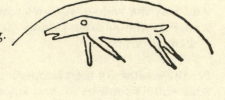

Dear Karl

Dear Karl, I send you Walt Whitman in a sixpenny book.
'How dilettante', I hear you observe, 'I hate these selections
Arbitrarily made to meet a need that is not mine and a taste
Utterly antagonistic, wholly alien, egregiously coercionary
Of individualism's, egotism's, insolence's light-fingered
    traffickings.'
Put a leash on your indignation; hold it on a tight short leash,
Muzzle it in a tough criss-cross mesh of temporization and
    impartiality.
'God, I have no such dishonourable merchandise, such tinsel
    and tawdry in my shop window.'
So you say. Then borrow or steal a muzzle to muzzle your
    indignation,
A criss-cross wire mesh of temporization and suavity, and with
    a muzzled and leashed wrath
Hanging on your tapping heels: Listen.
If I had what hypocritical poetasters crocodilely whining call
    lucre and filthy,
But man, and it takes a man to articulate the unpalatable truth,
Means of support, if I had this and a little more,
I would give you Leaves of Grass, I would send
All of Walt Whitman to you with a smile that guesses it is
More blest to give than receive.
For I, I myself, I have no Leaves of Grass
But only Walt Whitman in a sixpenny book,

Taste's, blend's, essence's, multum-in-parvo's Walt Whitman.
And now sending it to you I say:
Fare out, Karl, on an afternoon's excursion, on a sixpenny
   unexplored uncharted road,
Over sixpennyworth of tarmac, blistered by an American sun,
   over irrupted boulders,
And a hundred freakish geology's superimpositions. Fare out
   on a strange road
Between lunchtime and dinner. Bon voyage, Karl, bon voyage.

My Soul

In the flame of the flickering fire
The sins of my soul are few
And the thoughts in my head are the thoughts of a bed
With a solitary view.
But the eye of eternal consciousness
Must blink as a bat blinks bright
Or ever the thoughts in my head be stilled
On the brink of eternal night.

Oh feed to the golden fish his egg
Where he floats in his captive bowl,
To the cat his kind from the womb born blind,
And to the Lord my soul.

In My Dreams

In my dreams I am always saying goodbye and riding away,
Whither and why I know not nor do I care.
And the parting is sweet and the parting over is sweeter,
And sweetest of all is the night and the rushing air.

In my dreams they are always waving their hands and saying
    goodbye,
And they give me the stirrup cup and I smile as I drink,
I am glad the journey is set, I am glad I am going,
I am glad, I am glad, that my friends don't know what I think.

The Lads of the Village

The lads of the village, we read in the lay,
By medalled commanders are muddled away,
And the picture that the poet makes is not very gay.

Poet, let the red blood flow, it makes the pattern better,
And let the tears flow, too, and grief stand that is their begetter,
And let man have his self-forged chain and hug every fetter.

For without the juxtaposition of muddles, medals and clay,
Would the picture be so very much more gay,
Would it not be a frivolous dance upon a summer's day?

Oh sigh no more: Away with the folly of commanders.
That will not take a better song upon the field of Flanders,
Or upon any field of experience where pain makes patterns the
    poet slanders.

The River Humber

No wonder
The river Humber
Lies in a silken slumber.

For it is dawn
And over the newly warm
Earth the mists turn,

Wrapping their gentle fringes
Upon the river where it hinges
Upon the perfect sleep of perfected images.

Quiet in the thought of its felicity,
A graven monument of sufficiency
Beautiful in every line the river sleeps complacently.

And hardly the dawn distinguishes
Where a miasma languishes
Upon the waters' farther reaches.

Lapped in the sleeping consciousness
Of its waves' happiness
Upon the mudbanks of its approaches,

The river Humber
Turns again to deeper slumber,
Deeper than deeps in joys without number.

'. . . and the clouds return after the rain'

To the tune 'Worthy the Lamb'

In a shower of tears I sped my fears
And lost my heavy pain,
But now my grief that knew relief
Is sultried o'er again.

Of leaf and flower of that first shower
No memories remain.
The clouds hang down in heavy frown
But still it does not rain.

Happy the man of simple span
Whose cry waits on his pain,
But there are some whose mouths are dumb
When the clouds return again.

'I'll have your heart'

I'll have your heart, if not by gift my knife
Shall carve it out. I'll have your heart, your life.

I do not love you, Mother,
I do not love another,
Love passed me by
A long time ago,
And now I cry
Doh ray me fah soh.

Fallen, Fallen

The angel that rebellion raised
In moment of ecstatic rage
Is fallen, is fallen; his power is gauged.

Noted, by rote is had, the word is spoken.
Nothing remains but a falling star for a token,
A tale told by the fireside, a sword that is broken.

Will Ever?

Will ever the stormy seas and the surges deep,
Swinging from left to right over the world,
Stay in their idiot pacing, silently sleep
In a memorial silence of precreation?

Alas for the crafty hand and the cunning brain
That took from silence and sleep the form of the world,
That bound eternity in a measuring chain
Of hours reduplicate and sequential days.

Would that the hours of time as a word unsaid
Turning had turned again to the hourless night,
Would that the seas lay heavy upon the dead,
The lightless dead in the grave of a world new drowned.

Ceux qui luttent . . .

Ceux qui luttent ce sont ceux qui vivent.
And down here they luttent a very great deal indeed.
But if life be the desideratum, why grieve, ils vivent.

Fuite d'Enfance

I have two loves,
There are two loves of mine,
One is my father
And one my Divine.
My father stands on my right hand,
He has an abstracted look.
Over my left shoulder
My Divine reads me like a book.
Which shall I follow . . .
And following die?
No longer count on me
But to say goodbye.

A leur insu
Je suis venue
Faire mes adieux.
Adieu, adieu, adieu.

Mother, What Is Man? (1942)

—————————— * ——————————

Human Affection

Mother, I love you so.
Said the child, I love you more than I know.
She laid her head on her mother's arm,
And the love between them kept them warm.

Murder

Farewell for ever, well for ever fare,
The soul whose body lies beneath this stone!
'Tis easy said by one who had a care
Soul should doff flesh. That has another tone?
My hand brought *Filmer Smith* to this strait bed—
Well, fare his soul well, fear not I the dead.

Girls!

Girls! although I am a woman
I always try to appear human

Unlike Miss So-and-So whose greatest pride
Is to remain always in the VI Form and not let down the side

Do not sell the pass dear, don't let down the side,
That is what this woman said and a lot of balsy stuff beside
(Oh the awful balsy nonsense that this woman cried.)

Girls! I will let down the side if I get a chance
And I will sell the pass for a couple of pence.

Autumn

He told his life story to Mrs Courtly
Who was a widow. 'Let us get married shortly',
He said. 'I am no longer passionate,
But we can have some conversation before it is too late.'

Advice to Young Children

'Children who paddle where the ocean bed shelves steeply
Must take great care they do not,
Paddle too deeply.'

Thus spake the awful aging couple
Whose heart the years had turned to rubble.

But the little children, to save any bother,
Let it in at one ear and out at the other.

The Face

There is a face I know too well,
A face I dread to see,
So vain it is, so eloquent
Of all futility.

It is a human face that hides
A monkey soul within,
That bangs about, that beats a gong,
That makes a horrid din.

Sometimes the monkey soul will sprawl
Athwart the human eyes,
And peering forth, will flesh its pads,
And utter social lies.

So wretched is this face, so vain,
So empty and forlorn,
You well may say that better far
This face had not been born.

If I Lie Down

If I lie down upon my bed I must be here,
But if I lie down in my grave I may be elsewhere.

Conviction (i)

Christ died for God and me
Upon the crucifixion tree
For God a spoken Word
For me a Sword
For God a hymn of praise
For me eternal days
For God an explanation
For me salvation.

Conviction (ii)

I walked abroad in Easter Park,
I heard the wild dog's distant bark,
I knew my Lord was risen again,—
Wild dog, wild dog, you bark in vain.

Conviction (iii)

The shadow was so black,
I thought it was a cat,
But once in to it
I knew it

No more black
Than a shadow's back.

Illusion is a freak
Of mind;
The cat's to seek.

Conviction (iv)

I like to get off with people,
I like to lie in their arms,
I like to be held and tightly kissed,
Safe from all alarms.

I like to laugh and be happy
With a beautiful beautiful kiss,
I tell you, in all the world
There is no bliss like this.

Le Majeur Ydow

'Eh bien! Marche!', fit le Majeur Ydow,
'Any more gentlemen like that? *I'll see them off!*'

But there were no gentlemen really, only the phantoms
He warred with in his perpetual tantrums.

She Said ...

She said as she tumbled the baby in:
There, little baby, go sink or swim,
I brought you into the world, what more should I do?
Do you expect me always to be responsible for you?

Quand on n'a pas ce que l'on aime,
il faut aimer ce que l'on a——

Cold as no love, and wild with all negation——
O Death in Life, the lack of animation.

The Conventionalist

Fourteen-year-old, why must you giggle and dote,
Fourteen-year-old, why are you such a goat?
I'm fourteen years old, that is the reason,
I giggle and dote in season.

Distractions and the Human Crowd

Ormerod was deeply troubled
When he read in philosophy and religion
Of man's lust after God,
And the knowledge of God,
And the experience of God
In the achievement of solitary communion and the loss of self.
For he said that he had known this knowledge,
And experienced this experience,
Before life and after death;
But that here in temporal life, and in temporal life only, was
    permitted,
(As in a flaw of divine government, a voluntary recession),
A place where man might impinge upon man,
And be subject to a thousand and one idiotic distractions.
And thus it was that he found himself
Ever at issue with the Schools,
For ever more and more he pursued the distractions,
Knowing them to be ephemeral, under time, peculiar,
And in eternity, without place or puff.

Then, ah then, he said, following the tea-parties,
(And the innumerable conferences for social rearrangement),
I knew, and shall know again, the name of God, closer than close;
But now I know a stranger thing,
That never can I study too closely, for never will it come again—
Distractions and the human crowd.

Be Off!

I'm sorry to say my dear wife is a dreamer,
And as she dreams she gets paler and leaner.
'Then be off to your Dream, with his fly-away hat,
I'll stay with the girls who are happy and fat.'

Lady 'Rogue' Singleton

Come, wed me, Lady Singleton,
And we will have a baby soon
And we will live in Edmonton
Where all the friendly people run.

I could never make you happy, darling,
Or give you the baby you want,
I would always very much rather, dear,
Live in a tent.

I am not a cold woman, Henry,
But I do not feel for you,
What I feel for the elephants and the miasmas
And the general view.

Mother

I have a happy nature,
But Mother is always sad,
I enjoy every moment of my life,—
Mother has been had.

My Heart was Full

My heart was full of softening showers,
I used to swing like this for hours,
I did not care for war or death,
I was glad to draw my breath.

Croft

Aloft,
In the loft,
Sits Croft;
He is soft.

Rencontres Funestes

I fear the ladies and gentlemen under the trees,
Could any of them make an affectionate partner and not
tease?——
Oh, the affectionate sensitive mind is not easy to please.

The Governess

The milky love of this bland child
Her governess has quite beguiled,
And now they spend the hours talking,
Sometimes winding wool and sometimes walking.

The Repentance of Lady T

I look in the glass
Whose face do I see?
It is the face
Of Lady T.

I wish to change,
How can that be?
Oh Lamb of God
Change me, change me.

The Magic Morning

The boating party
Started at dawn from Clarté.
Lightly lightly they stepped into the green boat
(The Lady Marion has left behind her golden coat).
Marion d'Arcy and Charley Dake
Were the only ones. He rowed her upon the lake.
He rowed her across the lake until the green shallows
Paled in a waxen lily litter striped with swallows.
And now the morning sun flecks the dark trees
And lightly the mauve sedge moves in a little breeze.

Charley Dake loves the ducal girl
But her eyelids flick flick upon his thoughts' whirl.
Oh my ducal girl, cries Charley in a fit
Of love-spasm. He is Cupid-hit.
But the Lady Marion smiles and smiles
And so they go again upon the watery miles.

'Oh Charley, Charley, do not go upon the water'
Cries a friendly swan, 'with the Duke's daughter.
You wish to marry er, my boy-carrier? you can not support er
Oh do not go with the Duke's daughter.'

There is an island in the lake, old brick walled,
Where the laurestina climbs and is not spoiled.
What man will spoil the brick walls of their yellow brim?
Such a one as is nervy bold and grim.
(Such a one, says the swan, as has something in store for him.)

Flick flick the eyelids of the lady mark
Where a dark angel floats across her father's park.
All the green grass shivers in a warning,
Flee, Charley, flee the magic morning.

But Charley is folly-blind to the visitation
Of the dark angel of consternation.
Boldly he plucks a golden cup
Throws it in Marion's lap and does not look up.

Ah then the thunder peals and the waters bound
For who took the flower, the angel says, must be drowned.
So up rears the lake water and drags him underneath
Where in suffering he draws his last breath.
'Never more', cries the swan, 'shall Charley be seen,
He is underneath the waters of the mise-en-scène.'
(And 'Charley, Charley, Charley' cry the swan-instructed
    curlews
Ever after as they fly to their nests in the purlieus.)

But the ducal girl comes safe to land and takes her coat,
And goes off in the likeness of a slim stoat.

The Pleasures of Friendship

The pleasures of friendship are exquisite,
How pleasant to go to a friend on a visit!
I go to my friend, we walk on the grass,
And the hours and moments like minutes pass.

Happiness

Happiness is silent, or speaks equivocally for friends,
Grief is explicit and her song never ends,
Happiness is like England, and will not state a case,
Grief like Guilt rushes in and talks apace.

Satin-Clad

Satin-clad, with many a pearl,
Is this rich and wretched girl.
Does she weep? Her tears are crystal,
And she counts them as they fall.

Old Ghosts

By one half as much power as the Roman Centurion.
de Quincey

I can call up old ghosts, and they will come,
But my art limps,—I cannot send them home.

The Failed Spirit

To those who are isolate
War comes, promising respite,
Making what seems to be up to the moment the most successful
 endeavour
Against the fort of the failed spirit that is alone for ever.
Spurious failed spirit, adamantine wasture,
Crop, spirit, crop thy stony pasture!

The Recluse

My soul within the shades of night,
Like a languid plant with a fungoid blight,
Shone out in unearthly damp a bright white light;
Pashy the ground underfoot where I trod,
Musing as I passed of the nature of God,
But on my reverent reveries and fruitful plod
Of tear-strewn steps, like a wrathful rod
Fell the touch of a girl, young in years and officious
Who broke at once at a touch my chain of delicious
Melancholy. Away flew every ecstasy.
With ridiculous intention she drew me to the sun,
My soul's rich languors decried,
And, e'er I could chide, away did run,
Leaving my soul undone.
O too much sun, O wretched presumption,
O too little wisdom and too much compunction.

'I could let Tom go— but what about the children?'

Since what you want, not what you ought,
Is the difficult thing to decide,
I advise you, Amelia, to persevere
With Duty for your guide.

Torquemada

Uncle Torquemada,
does Beppo know about Jesus?

The Story of a Story (1946)

———————————— * ————————————

'I am so awfully stuck,' sighed Helen. 'You see it is a monologue, it is Bella's monologue, it is saying all the time how much she is thinking about Roland all the time, and thinking back, and remembering, and so on. It is like a squirrel in a cage, it goes round and round. And now I am stuck. Tell me, Ba, how can I come out of it to make a proper ending,—ah, that is difficult.'

The two girls were having lunch together in the Winter-garden, the potted palms were languid, but underneath the palms stood out like tropic flowers the keen dark faces of the yellow-skinned business men. Everybody was drinking strong bitter coffee that was served rather cold and soon became quite cold. The yellow of the skins and the yellow of the whites of the eyes of the business men spoke of too many of these cups of coffee drunk too often.

'You do not mean to say,' said Barbara, 'that you are writing a story about Roland and Bella?'

'Well, I am trying to,' said Helen, 'but it is very difficult, but I am doing my very best.' She sighed again. Oh, how difficult it was.

'But,' said Ba, 'you know that Roland will not like that.'

'Pooh, nonsense,' said Helen, 'he told me that he would not mind. But it is so difficult, but difficult, always so difficult to write.' Helen sounded rather desperate. 'It must be right,' she said, 'quite right.'

'But Roland,' said Ba again.

Helen began to look rather dreamy. 'Human beings are very difficult,' she said. 'You know, it is like the lady in Maurice Baring, she was one of these foreign countesses he has, and she was sitting at dinner next to an English writer. "And vat is it you write about, Mr So-and-So?" she said. "Oh, people," he said, "people." "Ah, people," said the countess, "they are very difficult."'

'But Roland . . .' went on Ba.

'I do wish you would stop saying "But Roland,"' said Helen. 'I tell you Roland said to me, "Helen, I suppose you will write a story about us." And I said, "Well, perhaps I shall, but it is very difficult." "Well, do," said Roland. "write whatever you like Helen, I shan't mind."'

'Ah,' said Ba, 'he only said that to trap you.'

'No, no,' said Helen, 'he could not be so base.'

That evening Ba tidied herself and went round to see Roland and Bella. Bella was not very pleased to see her. Bella was a warm-hearted person, but this girl was rather tiresome, she was *devoted* to Roland.

'I think I ought to tell you,' said Ba, 'that Helen is writing a story about you.'

This is how the war broke out, the war that was to carry so much away with it, the personal war, the war that is so trivial and so deadly.

Bella loved Helen.

'Oh, Helen, how could you do such a thing?'

'What thing is that, Bella?'

'Why, to write a story about Roland and me.'

'Oh, that,' said Helen, 'why that is very difficult. I am so terribly stuck, you know. It is difficult.'

'But Roland . . .' said Bella.

'How is Roland?' said Helen. Helen admired Roland very much for his fine intelligence, and because this fine intelligence was of the legalistic variety, very different from Helen's.

'Roland is furious,' said Bella, 'simply furious.'

'It is so frightfully difficult,' said Helen, 'to get it exactly right.'

'He says that if you do not give him your word that you will not publish the story he will not see you again.' Bella was now in tears, she loved Helen and she loved Roland. 'It is all so difficult,' she said, 'and Ba with her student-girl devotion does not help, and this story makes it all so difficult.'

'Yes, yes,' said Helen, 'it is difficult. I am most frightfully stuck.'

'You mean you are going on,' wept Bella. 'Oh Helen, how can you?'

'Well, that is just it, I do not know that I can. But,' said Helen, 'I shall try.'

'But Roland says . . .'

'Pooh, *that*. He cannot be so stupid.'

The two friends walked together across Hyde Park to Hyde Park Corner. Coming down the long grass path between the trees towards the statue of the great Achilles, Helen saw a horse drawing a cart full of leaves and bushes. 'Oh look, Bella, look,' she said. The horse had broken into a gallop, he drew the cart swiftly after him. He was a tall heavy animal, dappled grey and white, his long flaxen hair flew in the wind behind him, the long pale hair streamed on the gale that was blowing up between the April trees.

'What is it,' said Bella, who was in the middle of saying something about Roland. 'Well, what is it?'

'That horse,' said Helen.

'How can you look at a horse at such a moment? You want it both ways,' said Bella.

Helen looked at Bella and laughed. 'It is the moment to look at a horse.'

She went home and went on with the story. It was building up slowly, it was not so bad now, it was coming right.

When she had finished it she took it round to Lopez, who was also a writer. Lopez was a very clever quick girl, she had a brilliant quick eye for people, conversations, and situations. She read the story right through without stopping. 'It is very good, Helen,' she said, and then she began to laugh.

When Helen had gone Lopez rang up all the friends, and the friends of the friends, the people who knew Lopez and who knew Helen, and who knew Bella and Roland, and even those who knew the devoted girl Ba.

'Look,' said Lopez, 'Helen has written a most amusing story about Roland and Bella. It is very amusing, exactly right, you know.'

Everybody was very pleased, and the soft laughter ran along the ground like fire.

Cold and ferocious, Roland heard about it, coldly ferociously he sent messages to Helen. Bella came running, bringing the ferocious messages. 'Pentheus, ruler of this Theban land, I come from Kithairon where never melts the larding snow ...' Yes, it was like the Greek messengers who have the story in their mouths to tell it all. 'Where never melts the larding snow,' that was surely the cold Roland, so ferocious now and cold.

'He says,' cried Bella, 'that he will never see you again if you do not give him your word that never shall the story be published.'

'Pooh,' said Helen, 'we have heard about that. Very well then, I shall never see Roland again.' But she, too, began to cry. 'It is so easy,' she said, 'to close a door.'

'But he says,' went on Bella, 'that he will have his solicitor write to you, that he will have his secretary ring you up, that if the story is published he will at once bring a libel action against you.'

'It is so difficult to get these stories right,' said Helen, her thoughts moving off from Roland to the dear story that was now at last so right, so truly beautiful.

Bella shook her ferociously. 'Listen, Helen, he will bring a legal action.'

Helen began to cry more desperately and to wring her hands. 'He cannot be so base, indeed it is not possible, he cannot.' But now through the thoughts of the beautiful story, so right, so beautiful, broke the knowledge of the cold and ferocious Roland, that was now standing with a drawn sword.

'Ah, ah, ah,' sobbed Helen.

Bella put her arms round her. 'It is no good,' she said, 'no one and nobody has ever got the better of Roland.'

'But I love Roland,' said Helen, 'and I love you, and I even love the student girl Ba, and I love my story.'

'You want it both ways,' said Bella.

'There is no harm in this story,' wept Helen, 'and he is condemning it unseen. He has not seen it, it is soft and beautiful, not malicious, there is no harm in it and he is destroying it.'

'Roland,' said Bella, 'is a very subtle person, he is this important and subtle character.'

'For all that,' said Helen, 'he does not understand, he does not understand one thing, or know one thing to know it properly. He is this legalistic person.'

'He is the finest QC of them all,' said Bella.

'He knows nothing,' said Helen, and at once her thoughts passed from the benign and the happy, to the furtive, the careful, the purposeful and the defensive.

'You are childish about this story,' said Bella.

'You shall see that I am not.'

'What are you thinking of now?' said Bella, watching Helen and watching the ferocious intent expression on her face.

'I am thinking of Baron Friedrich von Hügel,' said Helen.

'Eh, who might he be, and what are you thinking about him?'

'I am thinking of what he said.'

'And what did he say?'

Helen screwed up her face and spat out the words, the terrible judging words. 'He said, "Nothing can be more certain than that great mental powers can be accompanied by emptiness or depravity of heart." He was thinking of Roland, be sure of it.'

Helen went home and knelt down and prayed, 'Oh, God,' et cetera. She was a Christian of the neo-Platonic school. She prayed that she might do the right thing about the story. This matter that had been so trivial was now running deep, deep and devilish swift. It was time to pray. She prayed that all might come right between herself and Roland and her dear friend, Bella. She knelt for a long time thinking, but it did not seem the right thing to do to suppress the story because of the threat of legal action and for the fear of it. But she knew that Roland could have no idea of this, he could have no idea of Helen but the idea that she was a friend of Bella's, a rattle, a literary girl, a desperate character, a person of no right sense or decency. 'But I will go on with it,' said Helen, and she began to cry again, and said, 'It will be the death of me.' For now the human feelings were running very swiftly indeed, and on the black surface of the hurrying water was the foam fleck of hatred and contempt.

She did not see Roland because she would not give him her word. Driven by Bella, whose one thought was that the story should not be published, because of the trouble that would follow, Helen cried, 'I will give my word in contempt, using his own weapon, for my word shall mean as much as his word meant when he said, "Write about us, write what you like, I shall not mind."'

Bella felt that her heart would break, the violence and the obstinancy of Roland and Helen would break it quite in two.

'He denies that he ever said such a thing.'

'But Bella, you heard him. You are coming out of the bathroom carrying the goldfish. You heard him, you told me that you heard him.'

'I heard him say, "Go ahead, write what you like," but it was a threat.'

Helen began to choke. 'It was no threat, he spoke most friendly, very open he was, he was treating me as a friend, he was anxious that it should be right.' She sighed and smiled and gave Bella a hug. 'It was difficult, but now it is right.'

She did not see Roland, but still she saw her dear friend, Bella. But always Bella was telling her of the affair, *Roland versus Helen*, and how the situation lay, and what Roland had said only yesterday, and what the part was that the girl Ba was playing.

The weeks went by, the story was now accepted and to be published. Nobody had seen the story as it now was, worked upon and altered with cunning and furtiveness and care and ferocity, it was now a different story, hedged and pared from legal action, but as good as it had ever been, good, shining bright, true, beautiful, but pared from legal action.

Helen prayed that the story might come safely through. The friends said that Roland would not bring an action, that he would not do it, that he was playing a game of bluff to frighten Helen, to make her withdraw the story.

But now Helen had the thought that she was dealing with a maniac, *a person who would go to all lengths*.

The danger of the situation and the care for it made her grow thin, and every time that she saw Bella the harsh cruel words of Roland were repeated, and what Ba had said was repeated, and all of it again, and again; and then again.

'Ba says that it is a good thing that she has done informing against you,' said Bella, 'for in this way the story will not be published, and everybody's feelings will be spared.'

'But the feelings and truth of the story will not be spared,' said Helen, and a bitter look came across her face. 'That does not matter I suppose?'

Bella tore on, 'Roland was saying only yesterday, "Helen will have to write a story to say how the story was not published," and he laughed then and said, "Helen must be taught a lesson," and he said, "Now that she has learnt her lesson I am willing to see her again."'

Helen put her head on the tablecloth of the restaurant where they were having lunch and wept, and she said: 'I wish Roland was dead.'

It was now Good Friday. Restlessly, sadly, Helen moved about the wide empty garden. The sun shone down through the fine ash trees and the lawn was bright green after the heavy rain. What a terrible day Good Friday is as the hour of twelve o'clock draws near. Her Aunt was at ante-communion, her sister at the mass of the pre-sanctified, but Helen would not go to church because she had said, 'I wish he was dead.' She went into the garden to fetch the book that she liked to read on Good Fridays and read:

> *The third hour's deafened with the cry*
> *Of crucify Him, crucify.*
> *So goes the vote, nor ask them why,*
> *Live Barabbas and let God die.*
> *But there is wit in wrath and they will try*
> *A Hail more cruel than their crucify.*
> *For while in sport he wears a spiteful crown,*
> *The serious showers along his decent face run slowly down.*

She thought of the crucifixion that was now at twelve o'clock taking place, and she thought that she, in her hatred of Roland and her contempt for him (because of the violence of the law that he threatened to use) had a part among the crucifiers, and she wept and hid her face, kneeling against the cold bark of the fine ash tree. 'The cruelties of past centuries are in our bones,' she cried, 'and we wish to ignore the sufferings of Christ, for we have too much of a hand in them. Oh I do not wish Roland dead, but what is the use to love him and to love my dear Bella? They will not receive it and the door is now closed. But even now,' she said, 'if I withdraw the story, and give my word that neither here nor in America—(for it was not only British Rights that Roland was asking her to give up)—shall the story be published, nor after his death, will that door be opened again and shall I be received? Oh, no, no'—Helen screamed and twisted and beat her head against the cold ash tree bark—'I cannot do this, and if I did never could it be the same between us, for it would be the act of a slave person, and no good thing.' And she knelt at the foot of the fine ash tree and prayed, 'Come, peace of God,' et cetera.

She went into the house and fetched out her writing pad and wrote to Bella: 'Dearest Bella, I think we had better not see each other for a bit. I like to think agreeably of you and Roland and even Ba, but I cannot do this now while I am seeing you, so we had better not see each other.' She paused and then went on, 'We can think of each other in the past as if we were dead.' Helen's face brightened at this idea, 'Yes, as if we were dead. So with love to you and Roland and Ba.'

When she had written her letter she thought, 'One must pay

out everything, but it is not happy.' She thought of Bella's beautiful house and the beautiful pictures that Roland had collected, especially there was such a beautiful picture in the hall, the Elsheimer, ah, that was it, *it was the gem of his collection*. Helen wept to think that never again would she see her dear friends, Roland and Bella, in love and friendship, and never again would she see the beautiful house, the Elsheimer, the trees in the shady garden or the goldfish swimming in their square glass tank. She thought that she must pay out everything and she supposed that the Grünewald prints that Roland had lent her must now also be given back.

She fell asleep in the garden and dreamt that she was standing up in court accused of treachery, blasphemy, theft and conduct prejudicial to discipline. Roland was cross-examining her:

'Do you think it is immoral to write about people?'

'No no, it is very difficult.' She held out her hands to Bella and Roland, but they turned from her.

'You go into houses under cover of friendship and steal away the words that are spoken.'

'Oh, it is difficult, so difficult, one cannot remember them, the words run away; when most one wants the word, it is gone.'

'You do not think it is immoral to write about people?'

'It is a spiritual truth, it is that.'

The dream-girl breaks down under cross-examination by the cold and ferocious Roland. She is cross, lost and indistinct.

'The story is beautiful and truthful,' she cries. 'It is a spiritual truth.'

The girl cries and stammers and reads from a book that she draws from her pocket, 'Spiritual things are spiritually discerned, the carnal mind cannot know the things of the spirit.' She weeps and stammers, 'Of the Idea of the Good there is nothing that can be spoken directly.' The dream-girl glances furiously upon the Judge, the Counsels for Defence and Prosecution, upon the tightly packed friends, who have come to see what is going on. She reads again. 'Let those be silent about the beauty of noble conduct who have never cared for such things, nor let those speak of the splendour of virtue who have never known the face of justice or temperance.'

There was now a mighty uproar in the court, but the dream-girl cries out high above the clamour, stuttering and stammering and weeping bitterly, and still reading from her book, 'Such things may be known by those who have eyes to see, the rest it would fill with contempt in a manner by no means pleasing, or with a lofty and vain presumption, as though they had learnt something grand.'

'He that hath yores to yore,' said the Judge, 'let him yore.' And he pronounced the sentence, 'You are to be taken to the place from whence you came . . .' The police constable and the wardress in the dock beside her took hold of her.

On the Tuesday after Easter there was a letter from Bella. 'How could you lump me with Ba?' she wrote.

Helen sat in her office, here were the proofs of the story come by post for correction. How fresh and remote it read, *there was no harm in it.*

Her employer, who was a publisher, came into the room where she was sitting, 'What's the matter, Helen?' he said, seeing the tears running down her cheeks.

She told him the story of the story.

'Look here, Helen,' said the employer, 'just you cut them right out, publish the story, tell him to go to hell.' Then he said, 'I am afraid the editor will have to be told.'

The moment, which had been so smiling when the employer first spoke, now showed its teeth. 'Of course, I don't expect he'll mind,' he said. But mind he would, thought Helen.

She took the bath towel from the drawer in her desk and held it in front of her face. 'The law of libel,' she said in a low faint voice, 'is something that one does not care to think about.' She pressed the towel against her face. 'It is everything that there is of tyranny and prevention.'

'Yes, yes,' said the employer, and walking over to the mantelpiece he pinched the dead lilac flowers that were hanging down from the jam jar, 'Yes.'

Helen wrote to the editor to tell him. He regretted that in the circumstances he could not publish the story.

When Helen got the editor's letter she wrapped the raincoat that Bella had given her tightly about her and walked along the rain swept avenue that led to the park. She sat by the bright pink peony flowers and she thought that her thoughts were murderous, for the combination of anger and impotence is murderous, and this time it was no longer Good Friday and the soft feeling of repentance and sorrow did not come to drive out the hatred. The rain fell like spears upon the dark green leaves of the peony plants and the lake water at a distance lay open to their thrust. It was not enough to know that the door against Roland and Bella was now locked tight, she must forget that there had ever been such people, or a door that was open to be shut. But how long would it take to forget, ah, how long, ah, that would be a long time.

'Syler's Green' (1947)

Now the whole of Syler's Green when we first went there was a very beautiful place to live in, especially for young children. There were fields to play in and shady country lanes, and farmhouses with their cows and the pigs and there was a toll gate, with its barred gate a-swing and a little house at the side of it for the toll-keeper. It was a long time ago you know, and a ripe September time with the autumn sunshine in the air and the rich smell of acorns and damp mould and the michaelmas daisies, especially there was the smell of the large rich michaelmas daisies that grew in the churchyard. Of course it wasn't always September or always sunny but that is how one is apt to remember past times, it is always a sunny day. This sunny time of a happy childhood seems like a golden age, a time untouched by war, a dream of innocent quiet happenings, a dream in which people go quietly about their blameless business, bringing their garden marrows to the Harvest Festival, believing in God, believing in peace, believing in Progress (which of course is always progress in the right direction), believing in the catechism and even believing in that item of the catechism which is so frequently misquoted by the careless and indignant . . . 'to do my duty in that state of life to which it shall please God to call me' (and not 'to which it has pleased God to call me'); believing also that the horrible things of life always happen abroad or to the undeserving poor and that no good comes from brooding upon them—indeed it is not wholesome to do so—although an interest in one's neighbours' affairs is only natural. And indeed how can society be wholesome if everything is not above board?— believing in fact a great deal of nonsense along with the sense.

And much we children cared about all this, indeed we never gave it a thought. We were far too busy with our wonderful deep exciting devilish woods, for devilish they seemed as we came into

them from the bright sunshine and dived into their dark
shadows, devilish and devilishly exciting. . . .

It is very fortunate to grow up as we grew up, in a quiet place that
has the appearance of going on being the same really for ever,
instead of growing up to wander homeless, to be driven homeless
from place to place, and to know hunger and to know what it is to
have no home and no parents, but to take as matters of course
that ruins are your home and that persons unrelated to you,
remote if friendly, and in uniform, are to direct your lives; as now
is the commonplace of Europe. . . .

But do you know sometimes in a black-dog moment I wish that
the great trees that I remember in my childhood and the even
greater trees and the dense forests that were in these parts long
long before I was born, would come again, thrusting up their
great bodies and throwing up the paving stones, the tarmac roads
and the neat rows of pleasant houses, and that once again it could
be all forest land and dangerous thickets where only the wolves
and the wild boars had their homes. And there in the green
depths of Scapelands Lake lay the body of Grendel with her arm
torn off. She is mourning her son, the Monster, slain by Beowulf.

Those gentle woods of my remembered childhood have had a
serious effect upon me, make no doubt about it.

Childhood and Interruption

Now it is time to go for a walk
Perhaps we shall go for a walk in the park
And then it will be time to play until dark
Not quite, when the shadows fall it is time to go home
It is always time to do something I am never torn
With a hesitation of my own
For always everything is arranged punctually
I am guarded entirely from the tension of anxiety
Walk tea-supper bath bed I am a very happy child really
And underneath the pram cover lies my brother Jake
He is not old enough yet to be properly awake
He is alone in his sleep; no arrangement they make
For him can touch him at all, he is alone,
For a little while yet, it is as if he had not been born
Rest in infancy, brother Jake; childhood and interruption come
   swiftly on.

The Holiday (1949)

————————————— * —————————————

'The Christian solution'

When I was talking to Tom one day, when he was in his good mood and talking freely, he said we were about due for a religious revival, and I said: O yes, there were already signs of it. And I told him I had recently been sent in for review *Grey Eminence*, *Screwtape Letters* and *Death and Life* by Father D'Arcy.

Well, said Tom, how did it go?

Well, I said, to begin with I felt exalted and relieved, to begin with the Christian solution seemed the one. Especially in *Eminence*, I thought, there is much to encourage. But then it fell away from me, it turned to exasperation. Tom, I said, it too much bears the mark of our humanity, this Christian religious idea, it is too tidy, too tidy by far. In its extreme tidy logic it is a diminution and a lie. These rewards and punishments, this grading, this father-son-teacher-pupil idea, it too much bears the human wish for something finished off and tidy, something one can grasp lovingly and tight, trusting to the Father, the Son and the Holy Ghost. It is the most tearing and moving thing, this wish to gain marks and approval, to plod on, with personal and loving chastisement, to infinity. This beating idea is also something that is always coming up. The truth is that people cannot bear not to be beaten.

I read Father D'Arcy's book in proof, said Tom. When I had finished it I said: I don't believe a word of it.

We both began to laugh.

It cannot be like this, I said, it is not possible.

'A bad school'

My sister was not always so happy in her schools. In her last school, it was in Wales, it was like a madhouse. There it was a mixed boy-girl school, with a young, diffident and obstinate headmaster. He thought that to do the wrong thing strongly is better than to do nothing, but only he was by nature so vacillating that he could not even make up his mind what was the wrong thing, but if he was not impeded by a rationalizing attempt, he would do the wrong thing with a splendid spontaneity.

The female sub-head in this school was a super thyroid who screamed and cried and made everybody so nervous. When the poor child was sick, she said: 'You cannot be sick here.' But where could he be sick? He was driven into the cold playground where the rain fell.

In the commercial class the little boy wrote a business letter: 'Sadly we see our customers falling away from us, but I hope that we shall always be friends. And so, with love.' But soon he was taught the business language, ah that one was not quite the business language, but soon he was corrected.

This school building had been condemned since a long time by the education committee. But the local council had the idea to keep expenses down, they were proud of their renown in this endeavour, they were indeed the cheapest in the kingdom for school rates.

So then the war comes, and of course nothing can be done.

And all the time the children were being whipped. And Pearl thought it might be possible to whip the Harrow children and the Eton children, who are well fed, fat, and have a social security, but that it should not be possible to whip poor thin boys who are hungry, no, that should not be possible, because it breaks them up, they cannot bear it, it has destroyed them.

During the war the little children of this condemned school sat for many days in the damp air-raid shelters, for in that part of the country, it was near a great west coast sea-port, the raids were very frequent. And the children's cloakrooms were often awash with rain water, and they could not change their shoes; they got real ill. And they were crammed for scholarships and tormented, though it was (the young schoolmaster thought) for their own good.

There was also the little boy that his parents wished to get a scholarship for Eton, so Pearl must coach him in Greek. He got meningitis, he is now dead.

This was a bad school, with so much hatred between the teachers, and I-don't-see-why-I-should-do-it and he-says and she-says.

Pearl became ill with bronchitis, perhaps it was a saving bit of psychology that did it. It was the end of that school for her, she came home.

'The post-war'

Caz, I cry, Caz. How long will the post-war last, Caz, shall we win the post-war, how does it go?

So so, said Caz, getting up with a smile. He sits down in the corner and gives Tiny a jog with his feet as he swings them up on to the seat. So so, we rub along, another ten years or so will see us over the worst. We are vacillating lazy and slow, but we have never in all our history for one moment entertained the idea that it might be a good thing to lose a fight. We are not a sophistical people and are saved the dangers that run with sophism; and our education has not yet succeeded in taking away from us the weapons of our strength—insularity, pride, xenophobia and good humour.

'Suburban and high-class children'

The children, I said hurriedly, the children in our suburb, are always white-haired, blue-eyed, fat, strong children, there is, I said, a very strong nordic strain in our suburb. The highlying air of these parts is favourable to strong children. You know, Caz, I went on, when I was in Kensington Gardens one day, coming down from the Round Pond to the statue of Physical Energy by G. F. Watts, I was noticing the children of South Kensington. Now this is noticeable, once I met a crocodile of them, out walking from some high-class baby school in the neighbourhood, now these children were thin, they appeared nervous and poorly nourished, their legs were like sticks; these legs were also, a most noticeable thing, very short from knee to ankle, that is bad. They walked listlessly, in a lackadaisical manner, they wore a great mixture of garments; a little girl, for instance, was wearing a hand-woven light fawn overcoat above a longer tartan kilt, she had a fairisle knitted tam on her head, her lips were broken out in sores for the cold east wind that was blowing at that time, she seemed a boarding-school not home-cared for child you know? Her long mouse-coloured hair hung lankly in straggles, her eyes were slightly stuck out, with red lids. No, she did not look well. Some of the little boys had wind-breaker jackets and short knickers made of this expensive hand-woven material. So the children strung along, staring vacantly about them, and hanging on to the arm—those who could get near her—of a nanny-governess brisk person. This was a middle-aged girl wearing her hair in a brisk bob childishly caught up with hairslides above a weather beaten visage. As a matter of fact there were several of these grown-up persons, so that nearly all the children had someone to hang on to. These children did not compare at all favourably with the children of our suburb. For dash, durability and an alert mind they did not compare. No, Caz, they did not. Their accents were prettier of course (I do not care very much for instance for the suburban pronunciation of 'daddy'—'dur-der-ie') but languid. 'Did you and Bobby enjoy staying with Mummy?' asked the naïve school-mistress person. 'Did we enjoy staying with Lois?' poses the bored and shattered child, 'perhaps rather, she drinks a bit you know and Paul's cheque didn't come, but perhaps rather, yes; we aren't supposed to particularly.' Bobby dissociates himself from the conversation.

'Voices against England in the Night'

But all the time at the back of my mind is the thought of the expedient crucifixion, the crucifixion of Christ by the Romans, by the governing Romans, and I thought of England again and of the voices against her, and how they are saying that England should go because she no longer governs; they say she does not govern, that she is like water shifting to her own course, that she is not strong like Rome. Oh, is she not? Is not this an envious and superficial argument? And I sighed again and thought of those voices against England and I thought of the poem I wrote called by this name, *Voices against England in the Night*:

England, you had better go,
There is nothing else that you ought to do,
You lump of survival value, you are too slow.

England, you have been here too long,
And the songs you sing now are the songs you sung
On an earlier day, now they are wrong.

And as you sing the sliver slips from your lips
And the governing garment sits ridiculously on your hips
It is a pity you are still too cunning to make slips.

Dr. Goebbels, that is the point,
You are a few years too soon with your jaunt,
Time and the moment is not yet England's daunt.

Yes, dreaming Germany, with your Urge and Night
You must go down before English and American might,
It is well, it is well, cries the peace kite.

Perhaps England our darling will recover her lost thought,
We must think sensibly about our victory and not be distraught,
Perhaps America will have an idea, and perhaps not.

But they cried, Could not England once the world's best
Put off her governing garment and be better dressed
In a shroud, a shroud. Oh, history turn thy pages fast.

And I said to Caz: We are leaving India, you know that we are
leaving India. All that we have now been saying is already in the
past, we are leaving India. It is a thing beyond thought in the
world's history, it is the first time since men grew to cities and
government, the first time that a great Power in the full flush of
the greatest victory that men have won, it is the first time that
such a Power has taken its vassal country, its under-nation for
three hundred years in liege, and given it freedom; it is the first
time a great colonizing Power, not driven by weakness but in
strength choosing to go, has walked out for conscience sake and
for the feeling that the time has come. That is the answer to the
voices in the night.

'This writing business'

Oh he says now, I think it is this writing business that makes you
so sad: Oh, it is that, on top of the war and after-the-war and
being in the middle of things without the turning point yet come,
that makes you cry. Oh, the writing business is very corrupting.
(Caz looks away over my head, looking seriously.) Well, he says,
look round at the writing people, what do you see, eh? You see

greed, envy, self-righteousness, being puffed up, and vanity.

Yes, I said hurriedly, that is so. I went to a meeting once, a meeting of writers, and do you know, Caz, a person got up and said that writers were the leaders of the world, the influencers, the leaders, they were those to whom the people looked in their ignorance and distress, to whom they looked for guidance and a way out. Ha, ha, ha, ahem.

Yes, says Caz in this drawling voice, I find that remarkable, for they cannot rule themselves, so how can they rule others, to guide them and show them a way out? Why, look at So-and-so, he said (mentioning by name a certain aged author, supposed to be great both as writer and influence, of a mandarin caste of mind, and a most noticeable bad conduct). There is a girl living with him, said Caz, and this girl submits to the most deplorable misbehaviour on the part of Snooks, she is both the victim of this misconduct and the condoner of it. But when one says: 'My dear Miss, how can you submit to those things, how can you bring yourself to it?' she says: 'I count it a privilege, not dearly bought, to live with this great Snooks and, through living with him, to meet, if only in a menial fashion, the great ones of this age. Why, these men are the Keats, the Shelleys, the Byrons, and the Tennysons of our days.' 'If you believe that, dear Miss,' I said, 'then you will believe anything.'

And he said that she should by all means read Snooks's poems, for there was in them much of value that a reader might pull out, but that when he sought to teach, to pronounce, to pontificate upon the moral plane, then let her beware. There is much beauty in his writing, he said, that may with profit be pulled out by the discriminating reader, but his opinions, as moral judgments, as a way of life. . . ? A man's actions and his conduct are grounded in his thoughts, and Snooks's actions and his conduct, being what they are, of what value are his thoughts? But this little fool, he said, would have none of it; the man Snooks was her idol, she must swallow him whole, not only his unappetising aging person, but also his opinions and his philosophy. Writers' books may, of course, hold useful matter, went on Caz (of which the writer himself is not always fully conscious), for all that the writers may be persons of low moral standing, not to be associated with by the fastidious, scum of the earth, indeed, of value only in their books, and only then by the sifting process of the judging mind of the reader. So that in one long book, said

Caz, there may be only two thoughts of beauty and of worth, and for these two thoughts the reader must plunge and dive. The writer himself is to be considered as a felon, put to hard labour in a solitary cell, his work scanned by the warders, that are his readers, scrutinized by them, and judged for what worth there may be in it.

There is exaggeration in what you say, I said, but there is truth in it, too, but there is in reality little need to take this severe action against the writers. They are in a way the scum of the earth, now too fêted, too set up, too beautified, but I can assure you, Caz, if the writers like to think they are persons of general influence and leadership, we need not grudge them the pleasure they derive from this notion, for there is in fact no substance in it; they are neither influencers nor leaders, they are indeed wholly unattended to. Nor can it be found, in the history of the whole world, that any writer has influenced the course of history, though by their written propaganda they may have advanced the causes already in existence which gained their approval and the use of their ready pens. Was Edward I a writer, who framed the laws of England, was Torquemada in his terrible zeal, was Wilberforce in his charity, was Nelson in his victories, was Newton, was Harley? Is the great scholar Coulton not foremost a churchman? The philosophers? you may object. But are they first and foremost properly to be considered as writers? The nonsense that I have heard spoken in certain quarters is not worth an answer. The answer is in the world that rolls before us.

Let them know where they stand, said Caz solemnly, and let them walk in humility, docile to their inspiration, dogged in its service. 'So to the measure of the light vouchsafed, shine Poet in thy place and be content.' In this way, and only in this way, may they attain to greatness. And when they have genius and are submissive to it, then indeed there is no saying where the spirit may not drive their poetry, their stories, their pictures, their sculpture. For this is the hard way of all the arts. If the artist chose the softer way of social or political prominence, his art suffers, he sins against it, he becomes indeed the scum of the earth. By the quality of their art they stand or fall, they are not otherwise to be considered.

'Everything is in fits and splinters'

Uncle, I say, I was reading the Proverbs last night, what I just quoted, they are very practical, but in some fashion also they make an unpleasant picture of a too practical, too self-advantageous virtue. The ones that are repeated so often, you know? Don't waste time talking to fools, don't chatter, don't go after strange women, don't stay in bed. Be a squirrel, be an ant, the improvident person shall have nothing to eat in the winter. Don't spare the rod, beat your children, beat sense into your little ones, etc. And above all, don't back bills for strangers. There is, of course, this real noble love of wisdom, this is very strong, but it is so often the wisdom of Polonius, 'looking out for Number One'. Uncle, a lot of gay and generous people, like Lopez for instance, chatter an awful lot, and borrow money, and are not ants or squirrels. It is necessary to be practical. But it is not the whole of wisdom, it is not, it is only a part. Everything in this world is in fits and splinters, like after an air raid when the glass is on the pavements; one picks one's way and is happy in parts. Uncle, one sometimes has the false thought that if one could go back to one's childhood, right back as far as was possible, one should say: Here I first began to be wrongly educated, here I first was going wrong, here I went along the wrong path. And so the thought springs up, very forceful, very strong: Ah, if I could get back to that point, now that I know what I do know, it would be different. But really I know that it would not, I remember the poem I wrote, it had the line, 'Prenatally biassed, grow worser, born bad'. Yes, Uncle, everything is different but everything is always the same.

My tears fall down so fast I cannot see the potatoes.

The Royal Dane

Now is come the horrible mome,
When I to my sulphureous home,
Must go'ome, must go'ome.

Harold's Leap (1950)

*

The Castle

I married the Earl of Egremont,
I never saw him by day,
I had him in bed at night,
And cuddled him tight.

We had two boys, twins,
Tommy and Roly,
Roly was so fat
We called him Roly-poly.

Oh that was a romantic time,
The castle had such a lonely look,
The estate,
Heavy with cockle and spurge,
Lay desolate.

The ocean waves
Lapped in the castle caves.

Oh I love the ramshackle castle,
And the room
Where our sons were born.

Oh I love the wild
Parkland,
The mild
Sunshine.

Underneath the wall
Sleeps our pet toad,
There the hollyhocks grow tall.

My children never saw their father,
Do not know,
He sleeps in my arms each night
Till cockcrow.

Oh I love the ramshackle castle,
And the turret room
Where our sons were born.

Harold's Leap

Harold, are you asleep?
Harold, I remember your leap,
It may have killed you
But it was a brave thing to do.
Two promontories ran high into the sky,
He leapt from one rock to the other
And fell to the sea's smother.
Harold was always afraid to climb high,
But something urged him on,
He felt he should try.
I would not say that he was wrong,
Although he succeeded in doing nothing but die.
Would you?
Ever after that steep
Place was called Harold's Leap.
It was a brave thing to do.

Touch and Go

Man is coming out of the mountains
But his tail is caught in the pass.
Why does he not free himself
Is he not an ass?

Do not be impatient with him
He is bowed with passion and fret
He is not out of the mountains
He is not half out yet.

Look at his sorrowful eyes
His torn cheeks, his brow
He lies with his head in the dust
Is there no one to help him now?

No, there is no one to help him
Let him get on with it,
Cry the ancient enemies of man
As they cough and spit.

The enemies of man are like trees
They stand with the sun in their branches
Is there no one to help my creature
Where he languishes?

Ah, the delicate creature
He lies with his head in the rubble
Pray that the moment pass
And the trouble.

Look he moves, that is more than a prayer,
But he is so slow
Will he come out of the mountains?
It is touch and go.

Man is a Spirit

Man is a spirit. This the poor flesh knows,
Yet serves him well for host when the wind blows,
Why should this guest go wrinkling up his nose?

The River God

Of the River Mimram in Hertfordshire

I may be smelly and I may be old,
Rough in my pebbles, reedy in my pools,
But where my fish float by I bless their swimming
And I like the people to bathe in me, especially women.
But I can drown the fools
Who bathe too close to the weir, contrary to rules.
And they take a long time drowning
As I throw them up now and then in a spirit of clowning.
Hi yih, yippity-yap, merrily I flow,
O I may be an old foul river but I have plenty of go.
Once there was a lady who was too bold
She bathed in me by the tall black cliff where the water runs cold,
So I brought her down here
To be my beautiful dear.
Oh will she stay with me will she stay
This beautiful lady, or will she go away?
She lies in my beautiful deep river bed with many a weed
To hold her, and many a waving reed.
Oh who would guess what a beautiful white face lies there
Waiting for me to smoothe and wash away the fear
She looks at me with. Hi yih, do not let her
Go. There is no one on earth who does not forget her
Now. They say I am a foolish old smelly river
But they do not know of my wide original bed
Where the lady waits, with her golden sleepy head.
If she wishes to go I will not forgive her.

The Ambassador

... known also among the Phoenicians as Casmilus
Lemprière

Underneath the broad hat is the face of the Ambassador
He rides on a white horse through hell looking two ways.
Doors open before him and shut when he has passed.
He is master of the mysteries and in the market place
He is known. He stole the trident, the girdle,
The sword, the sceptre and many mechanical instruments.
Thieves honour him. In the underworld he rides carelessly.
Sometimes he rises into the air and flies silently.

Persephone

I am that Persephone
Who played with her darlings in Sicily
Against a background of social security.

Oh what a glorious time we had
Or had we not? They said it was sad
I had been good, grown bad.

Oh can you wonder can you wonder
I struck the doll-faced day asunder
Stretched out and plucked the flower of winter thunder?

Then crashed the sky and the earth smoked
Where are father and mother now? Ah, croaked
The door-set crone, Sun's cloaked.

Up came the black horses and the dark King
And the harsh sunshine was as if it had never been
In the halls of Hades they said I was queen.

My mother, my darling mother,
I loved you more than any other,
Ah mother, mother, your tears smother.

No not for my father who rules
The fair fields of Italy and sunny fools
Do I mourn where the earth cools.

But my mother, I loved and left her
And of a fair daughter bereft her,
Grief cleft her.

Oh do not fret me
Mother, let me
Stay, forget me.

But still she seeks sorrowfully,
Calling me bitterly
By name, Persephone.

I in my new land learning
Snow-drifts on the fingers burning,
Ice, hurricane, cry: No returning.

Does my husband the King know, does he guess
In this wintriness
Is my happiness?

Do Take Muriel Out

Do take Muriel out
She is looking so glum
Do take Muriel out
All her friends are gone.

And after too much pressure
Looking for them in the Palace
She goes home to too much leisure
And this is what her life is.

All her friends are gone
And she is alone
And she looks for them where they have never been
And her peace is flown.

Her friends went into the forest
And across the river
And the desert took their footprints
And they went with a believer.

Ah they are gone they were so beautiful
And she can not come to them
And she kneels in her room at night
Crying, Amen.

Do take Muriel out
Although your name is Death
She will not complain
When you dance her over the blasted heath.

The Weak Monk

The monk sat in his den,
He took the mighty pen
And wrote 'Of God and Men.'

One day the thought struck him
It was not according to Catholic doctrine;
His blood ran dim.

He wrote till he was ninety years old,
Then he shut the book with a clasp of gold
And buried it under the sheep fold.

He'd enjoyed it so much, he loved to plod,
And he thought he'd a right to expect that God
Would rescue his book alive from the sod.

Of course it rotted in the snow and rain;
No one will ever know now what he wrote of God and men.
For this the monk is to blame.

Le Singe Qui Swing

To the tune of Green-sleeves

Outside the house
The swinging ape
Swung to and fro,
Swung to and fro,
And when midnight shone so clear
He was still swinging there.

Oh ho the swinging ape,
The happy peaceful animal,
Oh ho the swinging ape,
I love to see him gambol.

Pad, pad

I always remember your beautiful flowers
And the beautiful kimono you wore
When you sat on the couch
With that tigerish crouch
And told me you loved me no more.

What I cannot remember is how I felt when you were unkind
All I know is, if you were unkind now I should not mind.
Ah me, the power to feel exaggerated, angry and sad
The years have taken from me. Softly I go now, pad pad.

The Broken Friendship

'My heart is fallen in despair'
Said Easter Ross to Jolie Bear.
Jolie answered never a word
But passed her plate as if she had not heard.

Mrs Ross is took to her bed
And kept her eye fixed on the bed-rail peg
'When I am dead roll me under the barrow,
And who but pretty Jolie shall carry the harrow.'

Jolie Bear is gone away
Easter Ross's heart is broke,
Everything went out of her
When Jolie never spoke.

'Duty was his Lodestar'

A song

Duty was my Lobster, my Lobster was she,
And when I walked with my Lobster
I was happy.
But one day my Lobster and I fell out,
And we did nothing but
Rave and shout.

Rejoice, rejoice, Hallelujah, drink the flowing champagne,
For my darling Lobster and I
Are friends again.

Rejoice, rejoice, drink the flowing champagne-cup,
My Lobster and I have made it up.

The After-thought

Rapunzel Rapunzel let down your hair
It is I your beautiful lover who am here
And when I come up this time I will bring a rope ladder with me
And then we can both escape into the dark wood immediately.
This must be one of those things, as Edgar Allan Poe says
    somewhere in a book,
Just because it is perfectly obvious one is certain to overlook.
I wonder sometimes by the way if Poe isn't a bit introspective,
One can stand about getting rather reflective,
But thinking about the way the mind works, you know,
Makes one inactive, one simply doesn't know which way to go;
Like the centipede in the poem who was corrupted by the toad
And ever after never did anything but lie in the middle of the
    road,
Or the old gurus of India I've seen, believe it or not,

Standing seventy five years on their toes until they dropped.
Or Titurel, for that matter, in his odd doom
Crying: I rejoice because by the mercy of the Saviour I
    continue to live in the tomb.
What is that darling? You cannot hear me?
That's odd. I can hear you quite distinctly.

The Deserter

The world is come upon me, I used to keep it a long way off,
But now I have been run over and I am in the hands of the hospital
    staff.
They say as a matter of fact I have not been run over it's
    imagination,
But they all agree I should be kept in bed under observation.
I must say it's very comfortable here, nursie has such nice hands,
And every morning the doctor comes and lances my tuberculous
    glands.
He says he does nothing of the sort, but I have my own feelings
    about that,
And what they are if you don't mind I shall continue to keep
    under my hat.
My friend, if you call it a friend, has left me; he says I am a deserter
    to ill health,
And that the things I should think about have made off for ever,
    and so has my wealth.
Portentous ass, what to do about him's no strain
I shall quite simply never speak to the fellow again.

A Humane Materialist at the
Burning of a Heretic

When shall that fuel fed fire grown fatter
Burn to consumption and a pitter patter
Of soft ash falling in a formless scatter
Telling Mind's death in a dump of Matter.

Mr Over

Mr Over is dead
He died fighting and true
And on his tombstone they wrote
Over to You.

And who pray is this You
To whom Mr Over is gone?
Oh if we only knew that
We should not do wrong.

But who is this beautiful You
We all of us long for so much
Is he not our friend and our brother
Our father and such?

Yes he is this and much more
This is but a portion
A sea-drop in a bucket
Taken from the ocean

So the voices spake
Softly above my head
And a voice in my heart cried: Follow
Where he has led

And a devil's voice cried: Happy
Happy the dead.

Our Bog is Dood

Our Bog is dood, our Bog is dood,
They lisped in accents mild,
But when I asked them to explain
They grew a little wild.
How do you know your Bog is dood
My darling little child?

We know because we wish it so
That is enough, they cried,
And straight within each infant eye
Stood up the flame of pride,
And if you do not think it so
You shall be crucified.

Then tell me, darling little ones,
What's dood, suppose Bog is?
Just what we think, the answer came,
Just what we think it is.
They bowed their heads. Our Bog is ours
And we are wholly his.

But when they raised them up again
They had forgotten me
Each one upon each other glared
In pride and misery
For what was dood, and what their Bog
They never could agree.

Oh sweet it was to leave them then,
And sweeter not to see,
And sweetest of all to walk alone
Beside the encroaching sea,
The sea that soon should drown them all,
That never yet drowned me.

Wretched Woman

Wretched woman that thou art
How thou piercest to my heart
With thy misery and graft
And thy lack of household craft.

Lightly Bound

You beastly child, I wish you had miscarried,
You beastly husband, I wish I had never married.
You hear the north wind riding fast past the window? He calls me.
Do you suppose I shall stay when I can go so easily?

To An American Publisher

You say I must write *another* book? But I've just written this one.
You liked it so much that's the reason? Read it again then.

The Rehearsal

I always admire a beautiful woman
And I've brought you some flowers for your beautiful bosom.

Who Shot Eugenie?

We had ridden three days Eugenie and I
And kept hidden
By an unnecessary habitual caution
The papers of our commission.

How blank is the heart when on service bent
Empty of all but official content
So inappropriate is all individual consideration
So impossible in the individual a communal realization
Of states', peoples', any group-mind's preoccupation,
That a girl in the service of her country at war
Must have a mind as blank as a wall
Apt only to carry
The terms of her commission and hurry.

Eugenie and I in an open deserted country
Had travelled till nightfall of the third day
When putting our horses at a hedge at the top of a hill,
Up and over,
We found ourselves under cover
Of a mighty forest whose pines' green needles
Fallen carpeted the ground and silenced our horses' footfall.

Now night was entrenched and over our head the stars
Shone out their fitful rather disturbing light
That hardly served to penetrate the gloomy thread
Of the long forest ride we rode upon.

Why is it starlight so disturbs our kind
Dissipates the purposes of the human mind
Emptying familiar things of all significance
Setting the thoughts in an inconsequent dance
And making the loftiest and ruling of them sit mumchance?
I said no word of this to her nor she to me,
We were old campaigners both of us you see,
Only we rode, she as I, distracted
And the heart had gone out of us both and the virtue,
We rode in silence.

Hour by hour of the night we rode and the sickle moon
Clearing the feathered treetops soared overhead
And the path we followed led always towards the north,
Skirting a lake. We saw where the arms of trees
Old wood and rotten and allowed to rot and to fall
When it should have been chopped and cherished in the service
    of nations

(According to the best interpretation of King's Regulations)
Broke surface.
Over our shoulders from the right the moonlight shimmered
Down and across the waters of the forest lake
Making in semblance more sombre the shadowy margin.
We were glad to leave it, the sombre sinister pool,
And rode till daylight came and the cold dawn wind,
And the stars grew pale, and the moon sank down on the west.

In the gray of the early day we dismounted and watered our
    beasts,
And breakfasted there by the side of the cold clear spring,
And tethered our horses, and lay and rested and slept,
The sleep of exhaustion. And still no sound,
No least hurry or flurry of wild birds moving,
Spoke of the alien presence of human beings,
The forest enclosed us around and my dreams were always
Of ways without ending and passively hostile Nature,
Of forests deploying and advancing with the power of death
In the huddle of trees and the treacherous undergrowth.

The sun was hot on my face when I woke, and Eugenie was dead,
Shot, with a bullet through her head.
Yet every chamber in her revolver was full to plenty
And only in my own is there one that is empty.

Deeply Morbid

Deeply morbid deeply morbid was the girl who typed the letters
Always out of office hours running with her social betters
But when daylight and the darkness of the office closed about her
Not for this ah not for this her office colleagues came to doubt her
It was that look within her eye
Why did it always seem to say goodbye?

Joan her name was and at lunchtime
Solitary solitary
She would go and watch the pictures
In the National Gallery
All alone all alone

This time with no friend beside her
She would go and watch the pictures
All alone.

Will she leave her office colleagues
Will she leave her evening pleasures
Toil within a friendly bureau
Running later in her leisure?
All alone all alone
Before the pictures she seems turned to stone.

Close upon the Turner pictures
Closer than a thought may go
Hangs her eye and all the colours
Leap into a special glow
All for her, all alone
All for her, all for Joan.

First the canvas where the ocean
Like a mighty animal
With a really wicked motion
Leaps for sailors' funeral

Holds her panting. Oh the creature
Oh the wicked virile thing
With its skin of fleck and shadow
Stretching tightening over him.
Wild yet captured wild yet captured
By the painter, Joan is quite enraptured.

Now she edges from the canvas
To another loved more dearly
Where the awful light of purest
Sunshine falls across the spray,
There the burning coasts of fancy
Open to her pleasure lay.
All alone, all alone
Come away, come away
All alone.

Lady Mary, Lady Kitty
The Honourable Featherstonehaugh
Polly Tommy from the office
Which of these shall hold her now?
Come away, come away
All alone.

The spray reached out and sucked her in
It was a hardly noticed thing
That Joan was there and is not now
(Oh go and tell young Featherstonehaugh)
Gone away, gone away
All alone.

She stood up straight
The sun fell down
There was no more of London Town
She went upon the painted shore
And there she walks for ever more
Happy quite
Beaming bright
In a happy happy light
All alone.

They say she was a morbid girl, no doubt of it
And what befell her clearly grew out of it
But I say she's a lucky one
To walk for ever in that sun
And as I bless sweet Turner's name
I wish that I could do the same.

Not Waving but Drowning (1957)

———————————— * ————————————

Not Waving but Drowning

Nobody heard him, the dead man,
But still he lay moaning:
I was much further out than you thought
And not waving but drowning.

Poor chap, he always loved larking
And now he's dead
It must have been too cold for him his heart gave way,
They said.

Oh, no no no, it was too cold always
(Still the dead one lay moaning)
I was much too far out all my life
And not waving but drowning.

'What Is She Writing?
Perhaps It Will Be Good'

What is she writing? Perhaps it will be good,
The young girl laughs: 'I am in love.'
But the older girl is serious: 'Not now, perhaps later.'
Still the young girl teases: 'What's the matter?
To lose everything! A waste of time!'
But now the older one is quite silent,
Writing, writing, and perhaps it will be good.
Really neither girl is a fool.

The Blue from Heaven

A legend of King Arthur of Britain

King Arthur rode in another world
And his twelve knights rode behind him
And Guinevere was there
Crying: Arthur, where are you dear?

Why is the King so blue
Why is he this blue colour?
It is because the sun is shining
And he rides under the blue cornflowers.

High wave the cornflowers
That shed the pale blue light
And under the tall cornflowers
Rides King Arthur and his twelve knights.

And Guinevere is there
Crying: Arthur, where are you dear?

First there were twelve knights riding
And then there was only one
And King Arthur said to the one knight,
Be gone.

All I wish for now, said Arthur,
Is the beautiful colour blue
And to ride in the blue sunshine
And Guinevere I do not wish for you.

Oh Lord, said Guinevere
I do not see the colour blue
And I wish to ride where our knights rode,
After you.

Go back, go back, Guinevere,
Go back to the palace, said the King.
So she went back to the palace
And her grief did not seem to her a small thing.

The Queen has returned to the palace
Crying: Arthur, where are you dear?
And everyday she speaks of Arthur's grandeur
To the knights who are there.

That Arthur has fallen from the grandeur
Of his powers all agree
And the falling off of Arthur
Becomes their theme presently.

As if it were only temporarily
And it was not for ever
They speak, but the Queen knows
He will come back never.

Yes, Arthur has passed away
Gladly he has laid down his reigning powers
He has gone to ride in the blue light
Of the peculiar towering cornflowers.

A Dream of Comparison

After reading Book Ten of 'Paradise Lost'

Two ladies walked on the soft green grass
On the bank of a river by the sea
And one was Mary and the other Eve
And they talked philosophically.

'Oh to be Nothing,' said Eve, 'oh for a
Cessation of consciousness
With no more impressions beating in
Of various experiences.'

'How can Something envisage Nothing?' said Mary,
'Where's your philosophy gone?'
'Storm back through the gates of Birth,' cried Eve,
'Where were you before you were born?'

Mary laughed: 'I love Life,
I would fight to the death for it,
That's a feeling, you say? I will find
A reason for it.'

They walked by the estuary,
Eve and the Virgin Mary,
And they talked until nightfall,
But the difference between them was radical.

My Hat

Mother said if I wore this hat
I should be certain to get off with the right sort of chap
Well look where I am now, on a desert island
With so far as I can see no one at all on hand
I know what has happened though I suppose Mother wouldn't
    see
This hat being so strong has completely run away with me
I had the feeling it was beginning to happen the moment I put it
    on
What a moment that was as I rose up, I rose up like a flying swan
As strong as a swan too, why see how far my hat has flown me
    away
It took us a night to come and then a night and a day
And all the time the swan wing in my hat waved beautifully
Ah, I thought, How this hat becomes me.
First the sea was dark but then it was pale blue
And still the wing beat and we flew and we flew
A night and a day and a night, and by the old right way
Between the sun and the moon we flew until morning day.
It is always early morning here on this peculiar island

The green grass grows into the sea on the dipping land
Am I glad I am here? Yes, well, I am,
It's nice to be rid of Father, Mother and the young man
There's just one thing causes me a twinge of pain,
If I take my hat off, shall I find myself home again?
So in this early morning land I always wear my hat
Go home, you see, well I wouldn't run a risk like that.

Anger's Freeing Power

I had a dream three walls stood up wherein a raven bird
Against the walls did beat himself and was not this absurd?

For sun and rain beat in that cell that had its fourth wall free
And daily blew the summer shower and the rain came presently

And all the pretty summer time and all the winter too
That foolish bird did beat himself till he was black and blue

Rouse up, rouse up, my raven bird, fly by the open wall
You make a prison of a place that is not one at all.

I took my raven by the hand, Oh come, I said, my Raven,
And I will take you by the hand and you shall fly to heaven.

But oh he sobbed and oh he sighed and in a fit he lay
Until two fellow ravens came and stood outside to say:

You wretched bird, conceited lump
You well deserve to pine and thump.

See now a wonder, mark it well
My bird rears up in angry spell,

Oh do I then? he says, and careless flies
O'er flattened wall at once to heaven's skies.

And in my dream I watched him go
And I was glad, I loved him so,

Yet when I woke my eyes were wet
To think Love had not freed my pet

Anger it was that won him hence
As only Anger taught him sense.

Often my tears fall in a shower
Because of Anger's freeing power.

Fafnir and the Knights

In the quiet waters
Of the forest pool
Fafnir the dragon
His tongue will cool

His tongue will cool
And his muzzle dip
Until the soft waters lave
His muzzle tip

Happy simple creature
In his coat of mail
With a mild bright eye
And a waving tail

Happy the dragon
In the days expended
Before the time had come for dragons
To be hounded

Delivered in their simplicity
To the Knights of the Advancing Band
Who seeing the simple dragon
Must kill him out of hand

The time has not come yet
But must come soon
Meanwhile happy Fafnir
Take thy rest in the afternoon

Take thy rest
Fafnir while thou mayest
In the long grass
Where thou liest

Happy knowing not
In thy simplicity
That the knights have come
To do away with thee.

When thy body shall be torn
And thy lofty spirit
Broken into pieces
For a knight's merit

When thy lifeblood shall be spilt
And thy Being mild
In torment and dismay
To death beguiled

Fafnir, I shall say then,
Thou art better dead
For the knights have burnt thy grass
And thou couldst not have fed.

Songe D'Athalie

From Racine

It was a dream and shouldn't I bother about a dream?
But it goes on you know, tears me rather.
Of course I try to forget it but it will not let me.
Well it was on an extraordinarily dark night at midnight
My mother Queen Jezebel appeared suddenly before me
Looking just as she did the day she died, dressed grandly.
It was her pride you noticed, nothing she had gone through
    touched that
And she still had the look of being most carefully made up

She always made up a lot she didn't want people to know how old
    she was.
She spoke: Be warned my daughter, true girl to me, she said,
Do not suppose the cruel God of the Jews has finished with you,
I am come to weep your falling into his hands, my child.
With these appalling words my mother,
This ghost, leant over me stretching out her hands
And I stretched out my hands too to touch her
But what was it, oh this is horrible, what did I touch?
Nothing but the mangled flesh and the breaking bones
Of a body that the dogs tearing quarrelled over.

The Hostage

You hang at dawn, they said,
You've done nothing wrong but at dawn you will be hung.
You'll pass tonight in this cell
With Father Whatshisname. He'll look after you well.

There were two truckle beds in the room, on one sat Father W.,
Reclining against a bolster. The lady sat on the other.

I should like you to hear my confession, Father, I'm not of your
    persuasion
I'm a member of the Church of England, but on this occasion
I should like to talk to you, if you'll allow, nothing more,
Just a talk, not really a confession, but my heart is sore.
No, it's not that I have to die, that's the trouble, I've always
    wanted to
But it seems so despondent you know, ungracious too,

She sighed. Daughter, proceed,
Said the Father. I am here at your need.

Even as a child, said the lady, I recall in my pram
Wishing it was over and done with. Oh I am
Already at fault. Wonderful how 'bright' they keep,
I'd say of the other children, quite without rancour, then turn
    again to sleep.
Yet life is so beautiful. Oh the scenery.

Have you ever seen the sun getting up in the greenery
Of a summer day, in Norfolk say,
And the mild farm animals lumbering in the thistles.
Presently the Five-Thirty Milk in the station whistles,
You can hear the clank of the cans. In the wood
Trees dip to the stream, the fish rise up for food,
Snap, the old fly's caught. Et cetera. Oh it's busy,
Life bustles in the country, you know; it should be easy.
But I was outside of it, looking, finding no place,
No excuse at all for my distant wandering face.

When I came to London West-Eight, it was much the same
Oh the beautiful faces of others in the falling rain,
In the buses, no fuss there, no question they weren't at home,
Oh why should it only be I that was sent to roam?
I tell you, Father, I trod out the troughs of despair,
I'd rush out of doors in a fit, hurry, anywhere,
Kiss in my mind the darlings, beg them to stop . . .
Till the wind came up hard and blew my beauties off.
The wind blew hard. I snuffed it up and liked it,
Oh yes I liked it, that was the worst of it.

Of course I never dared form any close acquaintance.
Marriage? Out of the question. Well for instance
It might be infectious, this malaise of mine (an excuse?). Spread
That? I'd rather be dead.

But will the Lord forgive me? Is it wrong?
Will He forgive me do you think for not minding being hung,
Being glad it will soon be over.
Hoping he isn't the Ruler, the busy Lover,
Wishing to wake again, if I must at all,
As a vegetable leaning against a quiet wall,
Or an old stone, so old it was here before Man,
Or a flash in the fire that split our world from the sun?

I find nothing to instruct me in this in Holy Writ,
Said Father W., only, Remember life not to cling to it.

Well I don't you know, said the lady, then aware of something
   comical

Shot him a look that made him feel uncomfortable
Until he remembered she came from the British Isles,
Oh, he said, I've heard that's a place where nobody smiles.
But they do, said the lady, who loved her country, they laugh like
    anything
There is no one on earth who laughs so much about everything.

Well I see, said the Father, the case is complicated,
I will pray for you, Daughter, as I pray for all created
Meanwhile, since you want to die and have to, you may go on
    feeling elated.

Dido's Farewell to Aeneas

From Virgil

I have lived and followed my fate without flinching, followed it
    gladly
And now, not wholly unknown, I come to the end.
I built this famous city, I saw the walls rise,
As for my abominable brother, I don't think I've been too lenient.
Was I happy? Yes, at a price, I might have been happier
If our Dardanian Sailor had condescended to put in elsewhere.
Now she fell silent, turning her face to the pillow,
Then getting up quickly, the dagger in her hand,
I die unavenged, she cried, but I die as I choose,
Come Death, you know you must come when you're called
Although you're a god. And this way, and this way, I call you.

Away, Melancholy

Away, melancholy,
Away with it, let it go.

Are not the trees green,
The earth as green?
Does not the wind blow,
Fire leap and the rivers flow?
Away melancholy.

The ant is busy
He carrieth his meat,
All things hurry
To be eaten or eat.
Away, melancholy.

Man, too, hurries,
Eats, couples, buries,
He is an animal also
With a hey ho melancholy,
Away with it, let it go.

Man of all creatures
Is superlative
(Away melancholy)
He of all creatures alone
Raiseth a stone
(Away melancholy)
Into the stone, the god,
Pours what he knows of good
Calling good, God.
Away melancholy, let it go.

Speak not to me of tears,
Tyranny, pox, wars,
Saying, Can God
Stone of man's thought, be good?

Say rather it is enough
That the stuffed
Stone of man's good, growing,
By man's called God.
Away, melancholy, let it go.

Man aspires
To good,
To love
Sighs;

Beaten, corrupted, dying
In his own blood lying

Yet heaves up an eye above
Cries, Love, love.
It is his virtue needs explaining,
Not his failing.

Away, melancholy,
Away with it, let it go.

The Jungle Husband

Dearest Evelyn, I often think of you
Out with the guns in the jungle stew
Yesterday I hittapotamus
I put the measurements down for you but they got lost in the fuss
It's not a good thing to drink out here
You know, I've practically given it up dear.
Tomorrow I am going alone a long way
Into the jungle. It is all gray
But green on top
Only sometimes when a tree has fallen
The sun comes down plop, it is quite appalling.
You never want to go in a jungle pool
In the hot sun, it would be the act of a fool
Because it's always full of anacondas, Evelyn, not looking ill-fed
I'll say. So no more now, from your loving husband, Wilfred.

I Remember

It was my bridal night I remember,
An old man of seventy-three
I lay with my young bride in my arms,
A girl with t.b.
It was wartime, and overhead
The Germans were making a particularly heavy raid on
    Hampstead.
What rendered the confusion worse, perversely
Our bombers had chosen that moment to set out for Germany.
Harry, do they ever collide?
I do not think it has ever happened,
Oh my bride, my bride.

God the Eater

There is a god in whom I do not believe
Yet to this god my love stretches,
This god whom I do not believe in is
My whole life, my life and I am his.

Everything that I have of pleasure and pain
(Of pain, of bitter pain and men's contempt)
I give this god for him to feed upon
As he is my whole life and I am his.

When I am dead I hope that he will eat
Everything I have been and have not been
And crunch and feed upon it and grow fat
Eating my life all up as it is his.

The Airy Christ

After reading Dr Rieu's translation of St Mark's Gospel

Who is this that comes in grandeur, coming from the blazing
    East?
This is he we had not thought of, this is he the airy Christ.

Airy, in an airy manner in an airy parkland walking,
Others take him by the hand, lead him, do the talking.

But the Form, the airy One, frowns an airy frown,
What they say he knows must be, but he looks aloofly down,

Looks aloofly at his feet, looks aloofly at his hands,
Knows they must, as prophets say, nailèd be to wooden bands.

As he knows the words he sings, that he sings so happily
Must be changed to working laws, yet sings he ceaselessly.

Those who truly hear the voice, the words, the happy song,
Never shall need working laws to keep from doing wrong.

Deaf men will pretend sometimes they hear the song, the words,
And make excuse to sin extremely; this will be absurd.

Heed it not. Whatever foolish men may do the song is cried
For those who hear, and the sweet singer does not care that he
   was crucified.

For he does not wish that men should love him more than
   anything
Because he died; he only wishes they would hear him sing.

Dear Little Sirmio

Catullus recollected

Dear little Sirmio
Of all capes and islands
Wherever Neptune rides the coastal waters and the open sea
You really are the nicest.

How glad I am to see you again, how fondly I look at you.

No sooner had I left Bithynia—and what was the name of the
   other place?
And was safely at sea
I thought only of seeing you.

Really is anything nicer
After working hard and being thoroughly worried
Than to leave it all behind and set out for home
Dear old home and one's own comfortable bed?

Even if one wears oneself out paying for them.

'Great Unaffected Vampires and the Moon'

It was a graveyard scene. The crescent moon
Performed a devil's purpose for she shewed
The earth a-heap where smooth it should have lain;
And in and out the tombs great witches' cats
Played tig-a-tag and sang harmoniously.
Beneath the deathly slopes the palings stood
Catching the moonlight on their painted sides,
Beyond, the waters of a mighty lake
Stretching five furlongs at its fullest length
Lay as a looking-glass, framed in a growth
Of leafless willows; all its middle part
Was open to the sky, and there I saw
Embosomed in the lake together lie
Great unaffected vampires and the moon.
A Christian crescent never would have lent
Unchristian monsters such close company
And so I say she was no heavenly light
But devil's in that business manifest
And as the vampires seemed quite unaware
I thought she'd lost her soul for nothing lying there.

Nipping Pussy's Feet in Fun

(This is not Kind)

Oh Mr Pussy-Cat
My, you are sweet!
How do you get about so much
On those tiny feet?
Nip, nip; miaou, miaou,
Tiny little feet,
Nip, nip pussy-cat
My, you are sweet!

At School

A Paolo and Francesca situation but more hopeful, say in Purgatory

At school I always walk with Elwyn
Walk with Elwyn all the day
Oh my darling darling Elwyn
We shall never go away.

This school is a most curious place
Everything happens faintly
And the other boys and girls who are here
We cannot see distinctly.

All the day I walk with Elwyn
And sometimes we also ride
Both of us would always really
Rather be outside.

Most I like to ride with Elwyn
In the early morning sky
Under the solitary mosses
That hang from the trees awry.

The wind blows cold then
And the wind comes to the dawn
And we ride silently
And kiss as we ride down.

Oh my darling darling Elwyn
Oh what a sloppy love is ours
Oh how this sloppy love sustains us
When we get back to the school bars.

There are bars round this school
And inside the lights are always burning bright
And yet there are shadows
That belong rather to the night than to the light.

Oh my darling darling Elwyn
Why is there this dusty heat in this closed school?
All the radiators must be turned full on
Surely that is against the rules?

Hold my hand as we run down the long corridors
Arched over with tombs
We are underground now a long way
Look out, we are getting close to the boiler room.

We are not driven harshly to the lessons you know
That go on under the electric lights
That go on persistently, patiently you might say,
They do not mind if we are not very bright.

Open this door quick, Elwyn, it is break-time
And if we ride quickly we can come to the sea-pool
And swim; will not that be a nice thing to do?
Oh my darling do not look so sorrowful.

Oh why do we cry so much
Why do we not go to some place that is nice?
Why do we only stand close
And lick the tears from each other's eyes?

Darling, my darling
You are with me in the school and in the dead trees' glade
If you were not with me
I should be afraid.

Fear not the ragged dawn skies
Fear not the heat of the boiler room
Fear not the sky where it flies
The jagged clouds in their rusty colour.

Do not tell me not to cry my love
The tears run down your face too
There is still half an hour left
Can we not think of something to do?

There goes the beastly bell
Tolling us to lessons
If I do not like this place much
That bell is the chief reason.

Oh darling Elwyn love
Our tears fall down together
It is because of the place we're in
And because of the weather.

The Old Sweet Dove of Wiveton

'Twas the voice of the sweet dove
I heard him move
I heard him cry
Love, love.

High in the chestnut tree
Is the nest of the old dove
And there he sits solitary
Crying, Love, love.

The gray of this heavy day
Makes the green of the trees' leaves and the grass brighter
And the flowers of the chestnut tree whiter
And whiter the flowers of the high cow-parsley.

So still is the air
So heavy the sky
You can hear the splash
Of the water falling from the green grass
As Red and Honey push by,
The old dogs,
Gone away, gone hunting by the marsh bogs.

Happy the retriever dogs in their pursuit
Happy in bog-mud the busy foot.

Now all is silent, it is silent again
In the sombre day and the beginning soft rain
It is a silence made more actual
By the moan from the high tree that is occasional,

Where in his nest above
Still sits the old dove,
Murmuring solitary
Crying for pain,
Crying most melancholy
Again and again.

The Past

People who are always praising the past
And especially the times of faith as best
Ought to go and live in the Middle Ages
And be burnt at the stake as witches and sages.

My Heart Goes Out

My heart goes out to my Creator in love
Who gave me Death, as end and remedy.
All living creatures come to quiet Death
For him to eat up their activity
And give them nothing, which is what they want although
When they are living they do not think so.

Who is This Who Howls
and Mutters?

Who is this that howls and mutters?
It is the Muse, each word she utters
Is thrown against a shuttered door
And very soon she'll speak no more.

Cry louder, Muse, make much more noise
The world is full of rattling toys.
I thought she'd say, Why should I then?
I have spoke low to better men
But oh she did not speak at all but went away
And now I search for her by night and day.

Night and day I seek my Muse
Seek the one I did abuse
She had so sweet a face, so sweet a voice
But oh she did not make sufficient noise.

False plea. I did not listen then
That listen now and listen now in vain.

And still the tale of talent murdered
Untimely and untimely buried
Works in my soul. Forgive me, Lord, I cry
Who only makest Muses howl and sigh
Thou, Lord, repent and give her back to me
Weeping uncomforted, Lord have pity.

He did repent. I have her now again
Howling much worse, and oh the door is open.

Magna est Veritas

With my looks I am bound to look simple or fast I would rather
    look simple
So I wear a tall hat on the back of my head that is rather a temple
And I walk rather queerly and comb my long hair
And people say, Don't bother about her.
So in my time I have picked up a good many facts,
Rather more than the people do who wear smart hats
And I do not deceive because I am rather simple too
And although I collect facts I do not always know what they
    amount to.
I regard them as a contribution to almighty Truth, magna est
    veritas et praevalebit,
Agreeing with that Latin writer, Great is Truth and will prevail in
    a bit.

Jumbo

Jumbo, Jumbo, Jumbo darling, Jumbo come to Mother.
But Jumbo wouldn't, he was a dog who simply wouldn't bother
An ugly beast he was with drooping guts and filthy skin,
It was quite wonderful how 'mother' loved the ugly thing.

Farewell

Farewell dear friends
I loved you so much
But now I must leave you
And spread over me the dust

Fair life fare well
Fare never ill
Far I go now
And say, Farewell.

Farewell dear world
With the waters around you curled
And the grass on your breast
I loved you best.

Farewell fish and insect
Bird, animal, swift mover
Grim reptile as well
I was your approver.

Wide sky, farewell,
Sun, moon, stars in places
Farewell all fair universes
In far places.

Ding dong, ding dong
As a bell is rung,
Sing ding dong farewell
As a sweet bell.

'Cats in Colour' (1959)

Best of all, is the cat hunting. Then indeed it might be a tiger, and the grass it parts in passing, not our green English, or sooty town grass, but something high in the jungle, and sharp and yellow. But cats have come a long way from tigers, this tiger-strain is also something that can be romanticized. In Edinburgh's beautiful zoo, last summer with some children, I stopped outside the tiger's glass-bound cage. He was pacing narrowly, turning with a fine swing in a narrow turn. Very close to me he was, this glass-confinement needing no guard-rails. I looked in his cold eyes reading cruelty there and great coldness. Cruelty? . . . is not this also a romanticism? To be cruel one must be self-conscious. Animals cannot be cruel, but he was I think hungry. To try it out, to see whether I—this splendid human 'I'—could impinge in any way upon this creature in his ante-prandial single-mindedness, I made a quick hissing panting sound, and loud, so that he must hear it—hahr, hahr, hahr, that sort of sound, but loud. At once the great creature paused in his pacing and stood for a moment with his cold eyes close to mine through the protecting glass (and glad I was to have it there). Then suddenly, with my 'hahrs' increasing in violence, this animal grows suddenly mad with anger. Ah then we see what a tiger—a pussycat too?—driven to it, can do with his animal nature and his passion. Up reared my tiger on his hind legs, teeth bared to the high gums, great mouth wide open on the gorge of his terrible throat. There, most beautifully balanced on his hind legs he stood, and danced a little too on these hind paws of his. His forepaws he waved in the air, and from each paw the poor captive claws scratched bare air and would rather have scratched me. This great moment made the afternoon for me, and for the children too and for my old friend, their mama (and for the tiger I daresay) and cosily at tea afterwards in Fullers we could still in mind's eye see our animal, stretched and dancing for anger.

'My Muse' (1960)

Here are some of the truths about poetry. She is an Angel, very strong. It is not poetry but the poet who has a feminine ending, not the Muse who is weak, but the poet. She makes a strong communication. Poetry is like a strong explosion in the sky. She makes a mushroom shape of terror and drops to the ground with a strong infection. Also she is a strong way out. The human creature is alone in his carapace. Poetry is a strong way out. The passage out that she blasts is often in splinters, covered with blood; but she can come out softly. Poetry is very light-fingered, she is like the god Hermes in my poem 'The Ambassador' (she is very light-fingered). Also she is like the horse Hermes is riding, this animal is dangerous. . . .

Poetry does not like to be up to date, she refuses to be neat. ('Anglo-Saxon', wrote Gavin Bone, 'is a good language to write poetry in because it is impossible to be neat.') All the poems Poetry writes may be called, 'Heaven, a Detail', or 'Hell, a Detail'. (She only writes about heaven and hell.) Poetry is like the goddess Thetis who turned herself into a crab with silver feet, that Peleus sought for and held. Then in his hands she became first a fire, then a serpent, then a suffocating stench. But Peleus put sand on his hands and wrapped his body in sodden sacking and so held her through all her changes, till she became Thetis again, and so he married her, and an unhappy marriage it was. Poetry is very strong and never has any kindness at all. She is Thetis and Hermes, the Angel, the white horse and the landscape. All Poetry has to do is to make a strong communication. All the poet has to do is to listen. The poet is not an important fellow. There will always be another poet.

Selected Poems (1962)

―――――――――――――*―――――――――――――

Thoughts about the Person from Porlock

Coleridge received the Person from Porlock
And ever after called him a curse,
Then why did he hurry to let him in?
He could have hid in the house.

It was not right of Coleridge in fact it was wrong
(But often we all do wrong)
As the truth is I think he was already stuck
With Kubla Khan.

He was weeping and wailing: I am finished, finished,
I shall never write another word of it,
When along comes the Person from Porlock
And takes the blame for it.

It was not right, it was wrong,
But often we all do wrong.

May we inquire the name of the Person from Porlock?
Why, Porson, didn't you know?
He lived at the bottom of Porlock Hill
So had a long way to go,

He wasn't much in the social sense
Though his grandmother was a Warlock,
One of the Rutlandshire ones I fancy
And nothing to do with Porlock,

And he lived at the bottom of the hill as I said
And had a cat named Flo,
And had a cat named Flo.

I long for the Person from Porlock
To bring my thoughts to an end,
I am becoming impatient to see him
I think of him as a friend,

Often I look out of the window
Often I run to the gate
I think, He will come this evening,
I think it is rather late.

I am hungry to be interrupted
For ever and ever amen
O Person from Porlock come quickly
And bring my thoughts to an end.

                    *

I felicitate the people who have a Person from Porlock
To break up everything and throw it away
Because then there will be nothing to keep them
And they need not stay.

                    *

Why do they grumble so much?
He comes like a benison
They should be glad he has not forgotten them
They might have had to go on.

                    *

These thoughts are depressing I know. They are depressing,
I wish I was more cheerful, it is more pleasant,
Also it is a duty, we should smile as well as submitting
To the purpose of One Above who is experimenting
With various mixtures of human character which goes best,
All is interesting for him it is exciting, but not for us.
There I go again. Smile, smile, and get some work to do
Then you will be practically unconscious without positively
    having to go.

Thoughts about the Christian Doctrine
of Eternal Hell

Is it not interesting to see
How the Christians continually
Try to separate themselves in vain
From the doctrine of eternal pain.

They cannot do it,
They are committed to it,
Their Lord said it,
They must believe it.

So the vulnerable body is stretched without pity
On flames for ever. Is this not pretty?

The religion of Christianity
Is mixed of sweetness and cruelty
Reject this Sweetness, for she wears
A smoky dress out of hell fires.

Who makes a God? Who shows him thus?
It is the Christian religion does,
Oh, oh, have none of it,
Blow it away, have done with it.

This god the Christians show
Out with him, out with him, let him go.

Was He Married?

Was he married, did he try
To support as he grew less fond of them
Wife and family?

No,
He never suffered such a blow.

Did he feel pointless, feeble and distrait,
Unwanted by everyone and in the way?

From his cradle he was purposeful,
His bent strong and his mind full.

Did he love people very much
Yet find them die one day?

He did not love in the human way.

Did he ask how long it would go on,
Wonder if Death could be counted on for an end?

He did not feel like this,
He had a future of bliss.

Did he never feel strong
Pain for being wrong?

He was not wrong, he was right,
He suffered from others', not his own, spite.

But there *is* no suffering like having made a mistake
Because of being of an inferior make.

He was not inferior,
He was superior.

He knew then that power corrupts but some must govern?

His thoughts were different.

Did he lack friends? Worse,
Think it was for his fault, not theirs?

He did not lack friends,
He had disciples he moulded to his ends.

Did he feel over-handicapped sometimes, yet must draw even?

How could he feel like this? He was the King of Heaven.

... find a sudden brightness one day in everything
Because a mood had been conquered, or a sin?

I tell you, he did not sin.

Do only human beings suffer from the irritation
I have mentioned? learn too that being comical
Does not ameliorate the desperation?

Only human beings feel this,
It is because they are so mixed.

All human beings should have a medal,
A god cannot carry it, he is not able.

A god is Man's doll, you ass,
He makes him up like this on purpose.

He might have made him up worse.

He often has, in the past.

To choose a god of love, as he did and does,
Is a little move then?

Yes, it is.

A larger one will be when men
Love love and hate hate but do not deify them?

It will be a larger one.

My Muse

My Muse sits forlorn
She wishes she had not been born
She sits in the cold
No word she says is ever told.

Why does my Muse only speak when she is unhappy?
She does not, I only listen when I am unhappy
When I am happy I live and despise writing
For my Muse this cannot but be dispiriting.

The Frog Prince (1966)

———————— ✳ ————————

The Frog Prince

I am a frog
I live under a spell
I live at the bottom
Of a green well

And here I must wait
Until a maiden places me
On her royal pillow
And kisses me
In her father's palace.

The story is familiar
Everybody knows it well
But do other enchanted people feel as nervous
As I do? The stories do not tell,

Ask if they will be happier
When the changes come
As already they are fairly happy
In a frog's doom?

I have been a frog now
For a hundred years
And in all this time
I have not shed many tears,

I am happy, I like the life,
Can swim for many a mile
(When I have hopped to the river)
And am for ever agile.

And the quietness,
Yes, I like to be quiet
I am habituated
To a quiet life,

But always when I think these thoughts
As I sit in my well
Another thought comes to me and says:
It is part of the spell

To be happy
To work up contentment
To make much of being a frog
To fear disenchantment

Says, It will be *heavenly*
To be set free,
Cries, *Heavenly* the girl who disenchants
And the royal times, *heavenly*,
And I think it will be.

Come then, royal girl and royal times,
Come quickly,
I can be happy until you come
But I cannot be heavenly,
Only disenchanted people
Can be heavenly.

Phèdre

I wonder why Proust should have thought
The lines from Racine's Phèdre
    Depuis que sur ces bords les dieux ont envoyé
    La fille de Minos et de Pasiphaé to be
Entirely devoid of meaning,
To me they seem
As lucid as they are alarming.

I wonder why
The actresses I have seen
Playing Phèdre
Always indulge
In such mature agonising.
Phèdre was young,
(This is as clear in Racine as Euripides)
She was young,
A girl caught in a trap, a girl
Under the enforcement
Of a goddess.
I dare say Phèdre
In fact I'm sure of it
Was by nature
As prim as Hippolytus,
Poor girl, poor girl, what could she do
But be ashamed and hang herself,
Poor girl.

How awful the French actress
Marie Bell
Made her appear.
Poor Phèdre,
Not only to be shamed by her own behaviour,
Enforced by that disgusting goddess,
Ancient enemy
Of her family,
But nowadays to have to be played
By actresses like Marie Bell
In awful ancient agonising, something painful.

Now if I
Had been writing this story
I should have arranged for Theseus
To die,
(Well, *he* was old)
And then I should have let
Phèdre and Hippolytus
Find Aricie out
In some small meanness,
Say
Eating up somebody else's chocolates,
Half a pound of them, soft centred.
Secretly in bed at night, alone,
One after another,
Positively wolfing them down.
This would have put Hip. off,
And Phaedra would be there too
And he would turn and see
That she was pretty disgusted, too,
So then they would have got married
And everything would have been respectable,
And the wretched Venus could have lumped it,
Lumped, I mean, Phèdre
Being the only respectable member
Of her awful family,
And being happy.

I should have liked one member
Of that awful family
To be happy,
What with Ariadne auf Naxos,
And Pasiphaé and that awful animal,
And Minos sitting judging the Dead
In those awful dark halls.
Yes, I should like poor honourable simple sweet prim Phèdre
To be happy. One would have to be pretty simple
To be happy with a prig like Hippolytus,
But she was simple.
I think it might have been a go,
If I were writing the story
I should have made it a go.

'The Persian'

The gas fire
Seemed quite a friend
Such a funny little humming noise it made
And it had a name, too, carved on it you know,
'The Persian'. The Persian!
Ha ha ha; ha ha.

Now Agnes, pull yourself together.
You and your friends.

Emily writes such a good letter

Mabel was married last week
So now only Tom left

The doctor didn't like Arthur's cough
I have been in bed since Easter

A touch of the old trouble

I am downstairs today
As I write this
I can hear Arthur roaming overhead

He loves to roam
Thank heavens he has plenty of space to roam in

We have seven bedrooms
And an annexe

Which leaves a flat for the chauffeur and his wife

We have much to be thankful for

The new vicar came yesterday
People say he brings a breath of fresh air

He leaves me cold
I do not think he is a gentleman

Yes, I remember Maurice very well
Fancy getting married at his age
She must be a fool

You knew May had moved?
Since Edward died she has been much alone

It was cancer

No, I know nothing of Maud
I never wish to hear her name again
In my opinion Maud
Is an evil woman

Our char has left
And a good riddance too
Wages are very high in Tonbridge

Write and tell me how you are, dear,
And the girls,
Phoebe and Rose
They must be a great comfort to you
Phoebe and Rose.

Animula, vagula, blandula

The Emperor Hadrian to his soul

Little soul so sleek and smiling
Flesh's guest and friend also
Where departing will you wander
Growing paler now and languid
And not joking as you used to?

The Grange

Oh there hasn't been much change
At the Grange,

Of course the blackberries growing closer
Make getting in a bit of a poser,
But there hasn't been much change
At the Grange.

Old Sir Prior died,
They say on the point of leaving for the seaside,
They never found the body, which seemed odd to some
(Not me, seeing as what I seen the butler done.)

Oh there hasn't been much change
At the Grange.

The governess 'as got it now,
Miss Ursy 'aving moved down to the Green Cow——
Proper done out of 'er rights, she was, a b. shame.
And what's that the governess pushes round at nights in the old
    pram?

Oh there hasn't been much change
At the Grange.

The shops leave supplies at the gate now, meat, groceries,
Mostly old tinned stuff you know from McInnes's,
They wouldn't go up to the door,
Not after what happened to Fred's pa.

Oh there hasn't been much change
At the Grange.

Parssing there early this morning, cor lummy,
I 'ears a whistling sound coming from the old chimney,
Whistling it was fit to bust and not a note wrong,
The old pot, whistling The Death of Nelson.

No there hasn't been much change
At the Grange,

But few goes that way somehow,
Not now.

I love . . .

I love the English country scene
But sometimes think there's too much Hooker's green,
Especially in August, when the flowers that might have lent a
Lightness, don't; being gamboge or magenta.

Nodding

Tizdal my beautiful cat
Lies on the old rag mat
In front of the kitchen fire.
Outside the night is black.

The great fat cat
Lies with his paws under him
His whiskers twitch in a dream,
He is slumbering.

The clock on the mantelpiece
Ticks unevenly, tic toc, tic-toc,
Good heavens what is the matter
With the kitchen clock?

Outside an owl hunts,
Hee hee hee hee,
Hunting in the Old Park
From his snowy tree.
What on earth can he find in the park tonight,
It is so wintry?

Now the fire burns suddenly too hot
Tizdal gets up to move,
Why should such an animal
Provoke our love?

The twigs from the elder bush
Are tapping on the window pane
As the wind sets them tapping,
Now the tapping begins again.

One laughs on a night like this
In a room half firelight half dark
With a great lump of a cat
Moving on the hearth,
And the twigs tapping quick,
And the owl in an absolute fit

One laughs supposing creation
Pays for its long plodding
Simply by coming to this—
Cat, night, fire—and a girl nodding.

Voice from the Tomb

To the tune: 'From Greenland's icy mountains'
Hymns Ancient and Modern

I trod a foreign path, dears,
The silence was extreme
And so it came about, dears,
That I fell into dream,

That I fell into dream, my dear,
And feelings beyond cause,
And tears without a reason
And so was lost.

Cœur Simple

Where is the sky hurrying to
Over my head,
Mother, is the sky hurrying
To bed?

Where is the sky hurrying to
Over my head?
Where it will be hurrying to
When you are dead.

'What Poems Are Made Of' (1969)

Colours are what drive me most strongly, colours in painted
pictures, but, most strongly of all, colours out of doors in the fresh
cool air, the colours I see when I am walking in London streets, in
the country or by the sea....

Not all my poems come to me from what I watch and see and from
the colours I love. Many come from books I read (I almost never
read poetry), especially from the books I am sent for reviewing,
which are often books on controversial subjects, such as history
and theology. From the printed page, a counter-argument will
strike up in my mind. From this poems often come. There is
pleasure in this, but pain, too, because of the pressure on the
nerves; for all human beings it is like this. I love Death because he
breaks the human pattern and frees us from pleasures too
prolonged as well as from the pains of this world. It is pleasant,
too, to remember that Death lies in our hands; he must come if we
call him. 'Dost thou see the precipice?' Seneca said to the poor
oppressed slave (meaning he could always go and jump off it). I
think if there were no death, life would be more than flesh and
blood could bear.

Tom Snooks the Pundit

'Down with creative talent
(I have none)
Down with creative talent,
Kick it down!'

So cried Tom Snooks, a literary pundit,
The tender talent lay where he had stunn'd it,
He kicked the poor thing dead quite easily and then he cried:
'Hats off, my friends, it was a genius died.'

Oh long live Tom, long live his reputation,
(His proper name I'll give on application.)

Scorpion and Other Poems (1972)

———————————*———————————

Scorpion

'This night shall thy soul be required of thee'
My soul is never required of *me*
It always has to be somebody else of course
Will my soul be required of me tonight perhaps?

(I often wonder what it will be like
To have one's soul required of one
But all I can think of is the Out-Patients' Department——
'Are you Mrs Briggs, dear?'
No, I am Scorpion.)

I should like my soul to be required of me, so as
To waft over grass till it comes to the blue sea
I am very fond of grass, I always have been, but there must
Be no cow, person or house to be seen.

Sea and *grass* must be quite empty
Other souls can find somewhere *else*.

O Lord God please come
And require the soul of thy Scorpion

Scorpion so wishes to be gone.

How Do You See?

How do you see the Holy Spirit of God?
I see him as the holy spirit of good,
But I do not think we should talk about spirits, I think
We should call good, good.

But it is a beautiful idea, is it not?
And productive of good?

Yes, that is the problem, it is productive of good,
As Christianity now is productive of good,
So that a person who does not believe the Christian faith
Feels he must keep silent, in case good suffers,
In case what good there is in the world diminishes.

But must we allow good to be hitched to a lie,
A beautiful cruel lie, a beautiful fairy story,
A beautiful idea, made up in a loving moment?

Yes, it is a beautiful idea, one of the most
Beautiful ideas Christianity has ever had,
This idea of the Spirit of God, the Holy Ghost,
My heart goes out to this beautiful Holy Ghost,
He is so beautifully inhuman, he is like the fresh air.
They represent him as a bird, I dislike that,
A bird is parochial to our world, rooted as we are
In pain and cruelty. Better the fresh fresh air.

But before we take a Christian idea to alter it
We should look what the idea is, we should read in their books
Of holy instruction what the Christians say. What do they say
Of the beautiful Holy Ghost? They say

That the beautiful Holy Ghost brooded on chaos
And chaos gave birth to form. As this we cannot know
It can only be beautiful if told as a fairy story,
Told as a fact it is harmful, for it is not a fact.

But it is a beautiful fairy story. I feel so much
The pleasure of the bird on the dark and powerful waters,
And here I like to think of him as a bird, I like to feel
The masterful bird's great pleasure in his breast
Touching the water. Like! Like! What else do they say?

Oh I know we must put away the beautiful fairy stories
And learn to be good in a dull way without enchantment,
Yes, we must. What else do they say? They say

That the beautiful Holy Spirit burning intensely,
Alight as never was anything in this world alight,
Inspired the scriptures. But they are wrong,
Often the scriptures are wrong. For I see the Pope
Has forbidden the verse in Mark ever to be discussed again
And I see a doctor of Catholic divinity saying
That some verses in the New Testament are pious forgeries
Interpolated by eager clerks avid for good.

Ah good, what is good, is it good
To leave in scripture the spurious verses and not print
A footnote to say they are spurious, an erratum slip?

And the penal sentences of Christ: He that believeth
And is baptized shall be saved, he that believeth not
Shall be damned. Depart from me ye cursed into everlasting fire
Prepared for the devil and his angels. And then
Saddest of all the words in scripture, the words,
They went away into everlasting punishment. Is this good?

Yes, nowadays certainly it is very necessary before we take
The ideas of Christianity, the words of our Lord,
To make them good, when often they are not very good,
To see what the ideas are and the words; to look at them.

Does the beautiful Holy Ghost endorse the doctrine of eternal
    hell?
Love cruelty, enjoin the sweet comforts of religion?
Oh yes, Christianity, yes, he must do this
For he is your God, and in your books

You say he informs, gives form, gives life, instructs.
Instructs, that is the bitterest part. For what does he instruct
As to the dreadful bargain, that God would take and offer
The death of the Son to buy our faults away,
The faults of the faulty creatures of the Trinity?
Oh Christianity, instructed by the Holy Ghost,
What do you mean? As to Christ, what do you mean?

It was a child of Europe who cried this cry,
Oh Holy Ghost what do you mean as to Christ?

I heard him cry. Ah me, the poor child,
Tearing away his heart to be good
Without enchantment. I heard him cry:

Oh Christianity, Christianity,
Why do you not answer our difficulties?
If He was God He was not like us
He could not lose.

Can Perfection be less than perfection?
Can the creator of the Devil by bested by him?
What can the temptation to possess the earth have meant to Him
Who made and possessed it? What do you mean?

And Sin, how could He take our sins upon Him? What does it
    mean?
To take sin upon one is not the same
As to have sin inside one and feel guilty.

It is horrible to feel guilty,
We feel guilty because we are.
Was He horrible? Did He feel guilty?

You say He was born humble—but He was not,
He was born God——

Taking our nature upon Him. But then you say
He was perfect Man. Do you mean
Perfectly Man, meaning wholly? Or Man without sin? Ah
Perfect Man without sin is not what we are.

Do you mean He did not know that He was God,
Did not know He was the Second Person of the Trinity?
(Oh if He knew this and was,
It was a source of strength for Him we do not have)
But this theology of emptying you preach sometimes—
That He emptied Himself of knowing He was God—seems
A theology of false appearances
To mock your facts, as He was God whether He knew it or not.

Oh what do you mean, what do you mean?
You never answer our difficulties.

You say, Christianity, you say
That the Trinity is unchanging from eternity,
But then you say
At the incarnation He took
Our Manhood into the Godhead
That did not have it before,
So it must have altered it,
Having it.

Oh what do you mean, what do you mean?
You never answer our questions.

So I heard the child of Europe cry,
Tearing his heart away
To be good without enchantment,
Going away bleeding.

Oh how sad it is to give up the Holy Ghost
He is so beautiful, but not when you look close,
And the consolations of religion are so beautiful,
But not when you look close.
Is it beautiful, for instance, is it productive of good
That the Roman Catholic hierarchy should be endlessly
    discussing at this moment
Their shifty theology of birth control, the Vatican
Claiming the inspiration of the Holy Spirit? No, it is not good,
Or productive of good. It is productive
Of contempt and disgust. Yet
On the whole Christianity I suppose is kinder than it was,
Helped to it, I fear, by the power of the Civil Arm.

Oh Christianity, Christianity,
That has grown kinder now, as in the political world
The colonial system grows kinder before it vanishes, are you
    vanishing?
Is it not time for you to vanish?

I do not think we shall be able to bear much longer the dishonesty
Of clinging for comfort to beliefs we do not believe in,
For comfort, and to be comfortably free of the fear
Of diminishing good, as if truth were a convenience.
I think if we do not learn quickly, and learn to teach children,
To be good without enchantment, without the help
Of beautiful painted fairy stories pretending to be true,
Then I think it will be too much for us, the dishonesty,
And, armed as we are now, we shall kill everybody,
It will be too much for us, we shall kill everybody.

Nor We Of Her To Him

He said no word of her to us
Nor we of her to him,
But oh it saddened us to see
How wan he grew and thin.
We said: She eats him day and night
And draws the blood from him,
We did not know but said we thought
This was why he grew thin.

One day we called and rang the bell,
No answer came within,
We said: She must have took him off
To the forest old and grim,
It has fell out, we said, that she
Eats him in forest grim,
And how can we help him being eaten
Up in forests grim?

It is a restless time we spend,
We have no help for him,
We walk about and go to bed,
It is no help to him.
Sometimes we shake our heads and say
It might have better been
If he had spoke to us of her
Or we of her to him.
Which makes us feel helpful, until
The silence comes again.

Oh grateful colours, bright looks!

The grass is green
The tulip is red
A ginger cat walks over
The pink almond petals on the flower bed.
Enough has been said to show
It is life we are talking about. Oh
Grateful colours, bright looks! Well, to go
On. Fabricated things too—front doors and gates,
Bricks, slates, paving stones—are coloured
And as it has been raining and is sunny now
They shine. Only that puddle
Which, reflecting the height of the sky
Quite gives one a feeling of vertigo, shows
No colour, is a negative. Men!
Seize colours quick, heap them up while you can.
But perhaps it is a false tale that says
The landscape of the dead
Is colourless.

Archie and Tina

Archie and Tina
Where are you now,
Playmates of my childhood,
Brother and sister?

When we stayed in the same place
With Archie and Tina
At the seaside,
We used

To paddle the samphire beds, fish
Crabs from the sea-pool, poke
The anemones, run,
Trailing the ribbon seaweed across the sand to the sea's edge
To throw it in as far as we could. We dug
White bones of dead animals from the sandhills, found

The jaw-bone of a fox with some teeth in it, a stoat's skull,
The hind leg of a hare.

Oh, if only; oh, if only!

Archie and Tina
Had a dog called Bam. The silver-sand
Got in his long hair. He had
To be taken home.

Oh, if only . . . !

One day when the wind blew strong
Our dog, Boy, got earache. He had
To be taken home in a jersey.

Oh what pleasure, what pleasure!

There never were so many poppies as there were then,
So much yellow corn, so many fine days,
Such sharp bright air, such seas.

Was it necessary that
Archie and Tina, Bam and Boy,
Should have been there too?
Yes, then it was. But to say now:

Where are you today
Archie and Tina,
Playmates of my childhood,
Brother and sister? Is no more than to say:

I remember
Such pleasure, so much pleasure.

The House of Over-Dew

Over-dew
Became a dread name for Cynthia
In 1937
It was then that Mr Minnim first began to talk openly
About his dear wish.
How dear it was to be
For all of them!

Mr and Mrs Minnim had two sons
Who had done well at school
And won scholarships to Oxford.
Their boyhood was a happy time for all. Then
The elder son married Helen,
A fellow-student at the university,
And coming down, found a good post with sufficient money.
His wife also
Had money of her own, they were doing well.

The younger son, Georgie,
Was engaged to Cynthia. But that did not go so well.
He took a First in Greats, but then
The difficulties began. He could not find a job.
He did nothing, tried again; no good.
He grew sulky. It seemed hopeless.

It was now that the dread name of Over-Dew
Was spoken,
And a scheme bruited. It was this:
The Minnims were sincere and practising Christians, to
    Mr Minnim
Anyone who was not a Christian
Was a half-educated person.
It was, for instance, suggested
That his daughter-in-law should write a Life of St Benedict,
There was no good life of St Benedict, said Mr Minnim.
So Cynthia suggested that Helen should write it,
Because Helen was a Mediaeval History student,

Whereas Cynthia herself was a Latinist,
So why not Helen, with her special knowledge?
But Helen was not a Christian,
So, 'No', said Mr Minnim, she was a half-educated person.

The Over-Dew scheme was orthodox Christian.
When Mr Minnim retired from his accountancy work
He said that they should move from the suburb where they
    lived
And buy the house of Over-Dew, which was
A retreat for missionaries to have
On their leave-holidays in England.
And now it was being run, he said, in a fantastical fashion.

When they bought it
Everything would be better,
And different.
Where was the money to come from? No matter,
They had their savings, also they had the faith
Of Mr and Mrs Minnim.

Mrs Minnim loved her husband
And was pleased to follow him to the end of the earth, and
    certainly
Over-Dew was not that.

But oh when Cynthia heard that word
It was the knell
Of all her life and love. This, she said,
Is the end of happy days, and the beginning
Of calamity. Over-Dew, she thought,
Shall be the death of my love and the death of life.
For to that tune, she thought,
Shall come up a European war and personal defeat.

The Georgie situation
Was already sad. What could she do there?
                                        Nothing,
But see him and be silent and so enrage,
Or see him and speak, and the more enrage.

The wise and affectionate Cynthia
Must break the engagement and give back the ring.
There is nothing but this that she can do.
She takes up a post at London University
And in lecturing and study passes the days.
No more of that.

She has read a paper to her pupils
And fellow-dons, the subject is
The development of Latin from the first early growth
Upon the Grecian models. The study entrances,
She finds and reads a Latin prayer:
'I devote to Hades and Destruction'. It is a prayer
For time of battle, the thought is this:
I dedicate the enemy to Hades and Destruction.
                                        And perhaps
One or two of the praying Romans
Will devote also themselves
To Hades and Destruction. Rushing then into battle,
These 'devoted' people hope they may be killed.
                                        If not,
They are held for dead,
They are stateless, and in religion
Have no part at all. The gods have not accepted them,
They are alive, but yet they are destroyed.

In Cynthia's life, this sad year
Was twice as long as all the happy years before.
                                    She must now
Withdraw from Georgie and see him miserable.

She is at work and fast within her family,
The happy careless laughter
Of the brothers and sisters
Rings her round,
She has the home tasks, too,
And thinks of Georgie.

At the end of the year, in the bitter snow that fell that Christmas
The phrenzied Minnims
Moved from their life-long suburb.

The house of Over-Dew
Lay buried half in snow,
It stood five miles from any town upon a hillside.
Very bleak it was, and all the pipes were froze.
Mrs Minnim worked hard,
They had a girl to help them then she left.

Mrs Minnim had courage and was cheerful
But she was by now an old lady. Suddenly
There was the gift of a little money. Mr Minnim
Bought chasubles for visiting priests. But at first
There were no visitors at all, but only
The old cold house, and the lavatories frozen up
And wood kindling to be chopped and dried.
The work was bitter hard.
Mr Minnim, released suddenly
From the routine of his accountancy
Suffered in his head a strange numbness,
He moved about in a dream, would take no hand with the
    dishes.
    Even
When five-and-twenty missionaries came for a conference
He would do nothing.
He paced the garden plots, 'And here' he said,
'I will build twelve lavatories. And in this room
We will have a consecration and build an altar.'

The thaw came and turned all to mud and slush,
There was still no post for Georgie, he came down from Oxford
And washed the dishes for his mother,
And chopped the wood and moved also in a daze,
The immense learning
Lay off from him, the crude work of the house
Was an excuse from study.

But now Mrs Minnim was not happy, like a sad animal
She roamed the rooms of Over-Dew. This woman
Who had been so boisterous and so loving
With many friends, but still her own best thoughts
For Mr Minnim and their sons,
Was like a sad animal that cannot know a reason

Georgie, with the guilt of the excuse upon his heart,
Grew savage with her. The moody silences
Were shot with cruel words
It was so bitter cold within the house
Though now without the snow was melted and turned to
    slush.

The money situation preyed upon the mind of Mrs Minnim.

But her husband
Spoke of faith.

In the suburb where they once lived friends said:
How are the Minnims? Did you hear
That Mr Minnim had bought chasubles?

And then the foolish unkind laughter: Chasubles!
It will be
The ruin of them, the end.

There was one hope that Mrs Minnim had, it was this,
That they might return at last to their house in the suburb,
She had refused to let her husband
Sell this house. No, that she would not allow, No,
That must be for a return.

But now, out of this refusal was made
The bitterness of their life at Over-Dew. For, said her husband,
You kept back the seven hundred and fifty pounds
We might have had for selling the house.

In London
The girl who should have been Georgie's wife
Hears all; understands; loves Georgie; is helpless:
                                    reads to her class
The Latin prayer: I devote to Hades and Destruction.
She rules the harsh thoughts that run; cries;
'Come, love of God.'

Hendecasyllables

It is the very bewitching hour of eight
Which is the moment when my new day begins,
I love to hear the pretty clock striking eight
I love to get up out of my bed quickly.
Why is this? Because morning air is so cold?
Or because of new strength that seems to come then?
Both. And also because waking up ends dreams.

Black March

I have a friend
At the end
Of the world.
His name is a breath

Of fresh air.
He is dressed in
Grey chiffon. At least
I think it is chiffon.

It has a
Peculiar look, like smoke.

It wraps him round
It blows out of place
It conceals him
I have not seen his face.

But I have seen his eyes, they are
As pretty and bright
As raindrops on black twigs
In March, and heard him say:

I am a breath
Of fresh air for you, a change
By and by.

Black March I call him
Because of his eyes
Being like March raindrops
On black twigs.

(Such a pretty time when the sky
Behind black twigs can be seen
Stretched out in one
Uninterrupted
Cambridge blue as cold as snow.)

But this friend
Whatever new names I give him
Is an old friend. He says:

Whatever names you give me
I am
A breath of fresh air,
A change for you.

Come, Death (ii)

I feel ill. What can the matter be?
I'd ask God to have pity on me,
But I turn to the one I know, and say:
Come, Death, and carry me away.

Ah me, sweet Death, you are the only god
Who comes as a servant when he is called, you know,
Listen then to this sound I make, it is sharp,
Come Death. Do not be slow.

'On Writing'

Not very long ago I was reading this thing (The House of Over-Dew) and I thought, 'This is not prose, if falls into verse,' and I said, 'If it doesn't fall into verse I'm going to help it.'

There is no very strong division between what is poetry and what is prose.

(In a letter): . . . this will become a poem if I am not careful.

This is the unconscious poem that happens sometimes when people are talking.

Mr Eliot (in *Murder in the Cathedral*) uses banality with beauty in the Greek fashion that is so often parodied for an easy joke.

I take it that to judge well is one of the purposes of education, and how can you judge well if you are not grounded in the classics?

Differences between men and women poets are best seen when the poets are bad . . . But neither odd lives nor sex really signify, it is a person's poems that stand to be judged.

There can be no good art that is international. Art to be vigorous and *gesund* must use the material at hand.

Colours are what drive me most strongly.

A lot of the poems go to music—some of it my own and some other people's.

Hymn tunes, for instance, have a great influence on me.

What I shall do with your tunes is to get them so into my mind that some time a poem will fit itself to them, that is the way it does happen.

I am never very certain about them (the poems), the inspiration or whatever it is comes in such a vague and muddled way, and I am not sure that I don't sometimes get the wrong poems into print . . . and there are so many drawings, which I think are so much better than they used to be, and I can't get the poems to tie up to them.

I feel the drawings are so much a part of the verses that they must be published with them.

Oh, I've got a boxful of drawings . . . The drawings don't really have anything to do with the poems.

I went on re-reading *The Holiday*. Oh how much better I think it is than *Novel on Yellow Paper*. It is my favourite of everything I have written . . . I think it is *beautiful*, never brassy like N on Y P but so very richly melancholy like those hot summer days it is so full of that come before the autumn, it quite ravishes me now again when I read it, and the tears stream down my face. . . .

Why are so many of my poems about death, if I am having such an enjoyable time all the time?

There's a terrible lot of fear of life in my poems. I love life. I adore it, but only because I keep myself well on the edge.

How I wish my muse would not *only* respond to the disagreeable and sad.

These are all very moral poems, you know.

Notes

∗

Novel on Yellow Paper

'A foot-off-the-ground novel', p. 34
(*Novel on Yellow Paper*, pp. 38–40.)

'Those Victorian days', p. 35
(*Novel on Yellow Paper*, pp. 13–14.)
'To get the peculiar flavour of those days . . . you must read the novels of the period.' Her memory of reading *Mrs Haliburton's Troubles* and *Lost Sir Massingberd* in 'my paternal grandfather's library at Scaithness, Lincs' is the context for this passage.
'The woods decay . . .': Tennyson's *Tithonus*, first verse.
'the younger Tennyson': Harold Nicolson's *Tennyson* (1923) distinguishes 'Tennyson the poet' from 'Tennyson the bard' (chapter 1, 'The Tennyson Legend'), a division which became frequent.

'The German people', p. 35
(*Novel on Yellow Paper*, pp. 101–3.)
Pompey's visit in 1936 to the Eckhardt family in Berlin occasions a description of the atmosphere in Germany at the time. The two stories she refers to are from the Brothers Grimm.
'*Spieglein . . .*': 'Mirror, mirror on the wall, who is the fairest in the land?'
'*Frau Königin . . .*': 'Queen, you are the fairest here, but Snow-white is the fairest of all.'
'Sir Phoebus': Pompey's boss at the office (i.e., Sir Neville Pearson of Newnes and Pearson, for whom Stevie Smith worked as a personal secretary).
Wotan: Norse Odin, supreme God of Germanic mythology.

'The Bacchae', p. 37
(*Novel on Yellow Paper*, pp. 130–6.)
The context of this passage is a comparison of Euripides and Racine (cf. 'Phèdre' (p. 160) and note), and a satirical account of the sex instruction provided at Pompey's school by Miss Hogmanimy, whose warning that 'alcohol leads to irregularity in sexual behaviour' is contrasted with the second messenger's speech in the *Bacchae*: 'Take away wine and there is . . . no other joy, nothing left to man.'

The *Bacchae*, a late play by Euripides, shows Dionysus taking revenge on Thebes for the slander of his mother Semele. The women of Thebes, led by Agave, sister of Semele and mother of Pentheus, are driven mad by the god, who tricks Pentheus, King of Thebes, into pursuing them into the mountains dressed as a woman. They tear Pentheus to pieces. Dionysus orders that Agave (who has returned to her senses after killing her son) and the other women must go into exile.
'thyrsis': the wand of Dionysus, a staff wreathed with ivy.
'peplum': Greek woman's robe.

'The Church', p. 40
(*Novel on Yellow Paper*, p. 178–9.)
This passage concludes a long account of her difficulties in getting 'inside-of' the Christian religion. Cf. 'Was He Married?' (p. 154), 'Thoughts about the Christian Doctrine of Eternal Hell' (p. 154), 'How Do You See?' (p. 169).
Torquemada: the first Spanish inquisitor (?1420–1498) responsible for the burning of some two thousand heretics. See 'Torquemada' (p. 90), 'This writing business' (p. 108).

'A visitor', p. 41
(*Novel on Yellow Paper*, p. 212.)
Cf. 'In My Dreams' (p. 72), 'The Ambassador' (p. 114), 'Casmilus' (p. 60).
   See also *Novel on Yellow Paper*, p. 20: 'There's something meretricious, decayed, and I'll say, I dare say, elegant about Pompey. A broken Roman statue.'
   Stevie Smith's adoption of Hermes (Roman name Mercury) as a 'tutelary deity' explains her choice of 'Pompey Casmilus' as a fictional name in her first two novels. 'Casmilus' is another name for Mercury.
   Casmilus was one of the Cabeiri, obscure deities connected by the Samothracians with Hermes, and with a legend that Hermes and Proserpina were lovers. Hermes was the messenger of the gods, the patron of poets, thieves and merchants, the god of oratory, sleep and dreams, the inventor of the alphabet, music, numbers, weights, etc., and associated with fertility and with fighting. He was also the conductor of souls ('psychopompos') to the underworld. Janus, though, not Hermes, was the god with two faces who opened doors and looked both ways.
                    (Lemprière; *Oxford Companion to Classical Literature*)

A Good Time Was Had By All

Alfred the Great, p. 42
'Honour and magnify': 'We magnify thee and we worship thy Name', 1662 Prayer Book, *Te Deum*.

Egocentric, p. 42
The argument is reminiscent of Job's.
'nescient': ignorant.

Night-Time in the Cemetery, p. 45
first two lines: cf. A. E. Housman, 'About the woodlands I will go/To see
the cherry hung with snow.' (*A Shropshire Lad II*.)
'And hear the clank of jowl on jowl': cf. 'The clatter of jowl on jowl has
little aesthetic pleasure outside of the midnight fancies of Edgar Allan
Poe.' (*Over the Frontier*, p. 141.)

Infant, p. 45
Cf. *Novel on Yellow Paper*, pp. 162–3.

God and the Devil, p. 46
Cf. last verse of 'Thoughts about the Person from Porlock' (p. 153).
'bowels yearn': 'My bowels were moved for him', Song of Solomon 5:4;
'the bowels of compassion', 1 John 3:17.
'to point . . .': Johnson, *The Vanity of Human Wishes* 1.219 (on Charles XII
of Sweden), 'He left the name, at which the world grew pale,/To point a
moral, or adorn a tale.'

From the County Lunatic Asylum, p. 46
'spiritism': i.e., spiritualism.

Aubade, p. 48
'Aubade': dawn song.
'dam': mother.
'caesareanwise': cut out of the womb.
'the heavenly twins': sun and day.

The River Deben, p. 49
'The River Deben': a river in Suffolk. In *Over the Frontier*, pp. 113–14.
'Death sits in the boat with me': cf. Emily Dickinson, 'Because I could not
stop for Death'.
'Flow tidal river flow . . .': cf. Walt Whitman, lines such as: 'Smile O
voluptuous cool-breath'd earth ('Song of Myself', 21); 'Flow on, river!
flow with the flood-tide, and ebb with the ebb-tide!' ('Crossing Brooklyn
Ferry', 9); 'Come lovely and soothing Death' ('When Lilacs Last in the
Dooryard bloomed', 14).

Little Boy Lost, p. 50
In 'Syler's Green' (1947), *Me Again*, p. 98, as illustration of the effect of
'these woods of my childhood': 'Half wishing for them half fearing them,

it is like the poem I wrote about them.' Cf. 'Syler's Green' (p. 100).
   Cf. other 'fairy-tale' poems, e.g. 'The After-thought' (p. 119), 'The Magic Morning' (p. 86), 'The Castle' (p. 110), 'Fafnir and the Knights' (p. 134), 'The Blue from Heaven' (p. 129).
   Cf. Blake, 'The Little Boy Lost':
>   'Father, father, where are you going?
>   Oh do not walk so fast!
>   Speak, father, speak to your little boy,
>   Or else I shall be lost.'
>
>   The night was dark, no father was there,
>   The child was wet with dew,
>   The mire was deep, and the child did weep,
>   And away the vapour flew.

Bag-Snatching in Dublin, p. 51
In 'What Poems are Made Of' (1969), *Me Again*, p. 127, as illustration of how 'much there is to be seen in city streets that stirs the heart'.
'6/6': six-and-six (six shillings and sixpence).

Major Macroo, p. 52
'patient Griselda': the long-suffering heroine of Chaucer's 'The Clerk's Tale' in *The Canterbury Tales*.
'They went into every room . . .': a reminder of Bluebeard's castle.

All Things Pass, p. 53
Cf. 'All flesh is as grass, and all the glory of man is as the flowers of grass. The grass withereth, and the flower thereof falleth away.' 1 Peter 1:24.

Private Means is Dead, p. 53
Original title, 'Chaps'.
'Portion . . . person': cf. the play on Porlock/person/Porson in 'Thoughts about the Person from Porlock' (p. 152).

Breughel, p. 55
In 'Syler's Green' (1947), *Me Again*, pp. 87–8: 'The memory of these graveyard excursions fired me later on to write a very solemn poem indeed, which, for a reason I do not remember, I called "Breughel".'
   Cf. the description of a desolate wartime landscape in *The Holiday*, p. 198, (influenced by Browning's *Childe Roland*) referred to as 'by Breughel out of Hecate'.
   See 'Everything is in fits and splinters' (p. 109).
Metre: cf. Blake's 'Mad Song' ('The wild winds weep/And the night is a-cold').

Over the Frontier

'Georg Grosz', p. 56
(*Over the Frontier*, pp. 10–18.)
Georg Grosz: (1893–1959). Famous for satirical drawings and paintings of German society and for anti-war paintings. Born Berlin, went to New York in 1933; later paintings in a more romantic style. Returned to Berlin in 1959. Stevie Smith uses him (like the Eckhardt family in *Novel on Yellow Paper*) as an illustration of German culture and of England's attitude to Germany in 1938.
'Hohe Schule': *haute école*, the classical art of riding.
'fin de siècle': 1890s; aesthetic and, by implication, decadent.
Aubrey Beardsley: (1872–1898). Exotic, perverse, decadent illustrations as in *The Yellow Book* in the 1890s.
'*smoking*': i.e., dinner jacket.
'tendre': desire, yen.
'Gefühl': feeling.
RM: Reichmark.
Baden-Powell: (1857–1941). Lord Baden-Powell and his sister founded the Boy Scouts and the Girl Guides.
'*eine seelische Entlassung*': a release of emotions.
'somebody else's cup of tea': Christ's prayer in the Garden of Gethsemane, 'May this cup pass from me' is (very characteristically) turned into a politely English rejection.

'Casmilus', p 60
(*Over the Frontier*, pp. 87–8.)
See note to 'A visitor' (p. 41).
'the girl from Enna': see 'Persephone' (p. 114).
Minos and Rhadamanthus: with Pluto, the three judges of the dead.
Punic: Phoenician or Carthaginian.
Styx and Phlegethon: rivers of the underworld.

'Professor Dryasdust and Pater', p. 61
(*Over the Frontier*, pp. 89–94.)
'Dryasdust': the name given by Walter Scott to the fictitious 'reverend Doctor' of his prefaces; used by Carlyle and others to mean any plodding, prosy antiquarian or authority.
   Stevie Smith enjoyed satirizing academics, literary authorities, London intelligentsia, etc. This episode (like 'The Story of a Story' (p. 91), obviously taken from life) in which the pompous young Edinburgh academic reads Pater is also an occasion for debunking Anglo-Catholicism and *fin-de-siècle* aestheticism.
Belloc: Hilaire Belloc (1870–1953). English Roman Catholic writer.

Beachcomber: *Daily Express* column written by Wyndham Lewis (1919–24) and then by J. B. Morton.

Paracelsus: Renaissance Swiss natural philosopher, discovered the *summum bonum*, and is the subject of Browning's long poem.

'peinliches': painful.

Stratford Canning: (1786–1880). Cousin of George Canning: ambassador to Turkey in years leading up to the Crimean War.

'And the eyelids are a little weary': from Pater's description of the Mona Lisa, 'Leonardo da Vinci', *The Renaissance* (1873).

'To win the applause of schoolboys . . .': 'Ut pueris placeas et declamatio fias', Juvenal, *Satires*, X, 166.

When I Awake, p. 63
(*Over the Frontier*, p. 61.)
In the middle of an anguished passage about the 'cruelty' of 1936. In *Over the Frontier* the last two lines read: 'Come pounce, And take,/And make, An end at once.'

'Married to a tiger', p. 64
(*Over the Frontier*, p. 215.)
'Bottle Green': the name for Palmers Green, where she lived for most of her life, in her first two novels. She calls it 'Syler's Green' in the essay of that name.

'Power', p. 64
(*Over the Frontier*, pp. 271–2.)
Over the Frontier ends with this passage, in which she concludes that death is no solution; the only thing to set against power is love.
'ignis fatuus': will-o'-the-wisp.

Tender Only To One

O Happy Dogs of England, p. 65
In 'Syler's Green' (1947), *Me Again*, p. 96: 'It is about the dogs of Syler's Green that I wrote my poem called "The Dogs of England".' In *Me Again*, line 2 reads 'Bark well as bark you may'.

In a BBC reading (29 November 1968) she describes the poem as 'political and heaven knows relevant'.

The Bishops of the Church of England, p. 66
Cf. *Novel on Yellow Paper*, p. 35: 'I admire the bishops of the Church of England and I often think about them and think they must get a laugh to see the way the R.C.'s go round about trying like holy smoke to undermine them. . . . It's impossible to be a bishop of the Church of England and a fool.'

One of Many, p. 66
Several references are mixed together in this poem. In *Over the Frontier*,
pp. 52–3, she talks about Hardy's poem 'Midnight on the Great Western'
(which she calls 'The Boy in the Third Class Railway Carriage') and the
boy, 'Father Time', in Hardy's *Jude the Obscure*, who hangs himself and
his siblings 'because we are too menny'. In Blake's 'A Little Boy Lost', the
priest burns the child for setting 'reason up for judge/Of our most holy
mystery'. In Lewis Carroll's *Alice's Adventures in Wonderland*, Old Fury is
the cat in the mouse's poem:

> I'll be judge, I'll be jury
> Said cunning Old Fury:
> I'll try the whole case
> And condemn you to death.

The Doctor, p. 67
'bromide': a tranquillizer.

Silence and Tears, p. 68
In 'A Turn Outside' (BBC dialogue between Stevie Smith and an
interlocutor, 23 May 1959), *Me Again*, p. 337: 'The idea of the poem is that
there is a funeral service going on in the rain. It was inspired by an
advertisement I saw in a clerical outfitters' catalogue.... It's "The Death
of Poor Cock Robin" tune.'

Dear Karl, p. 70
Karl: Pompey's German boyfriend in *Novel on Yellow Paper*.
'Leaves of Grass': Walt Whitman's long book of poems, which
developed through gradual stages of publication between 1855 and 1882,
and was reprinted in many editions and selections.
'multum-in-parvo': much in a small space.
'Fare out . . .': cf. 'Allons! The road is before us!', Whitman, 'Song of the
Open Road', 15.

In My Dreams, p. 72
In *Over the Frontier*, the context is Pompey's mysterious wartime mission,
and the poem is contrasted with Titurel's 'coming to terms with a
life-in-death existence' (see note to 'The After-thought' (p. 119)). In *Over
the Frontier*, line 3 reads 'And the parting is sweet and the parting over is
sweetest'.
Cf. 'A visitor' (p. 41).

The Lads of the Village, p. 72
'self-forged chain': cf. Blake's 'London', 'mind-forged manacles'.
Flanders: major battlefield of First World War.
Collected Poems has 'sing' for 'sigh' and 'This will not make' in line 11.

'. . . and the clouds return after the rain', p. 74
The quotation should read: 'While the sun, or the light, or the moon, or the stars, be not darkened, nor the clouds return after the rain', *Ecclesiastes* 12:1. (See *Me Again*, p. 208: a 'great key passage'.)
    Cf. Blake's 'Christian Forbearance':

> I was angry with my friend:
> I told my wrath, my wrath did end.
> I was angry with my foe:
> I told it not, my wrath did grow.

The River Humber, p. 73
'The River Humber': estuary in NE England, flows east into the North Sea. (Stevie Smith was born in Hull.)

'I'll have your heart', p. 74
Original title, 'Tu refuses à obeir à ta mère . . .!'
    In 'What Poems are Made Of' (1969), *Me Again*, p. 129: 'I imagine this: that a little child has been turned to stone in his mother's lap. She clutches him and cries: "I'll have", etc.'
    In *The Holiday*, p. 62: 'It is the desire to tear out this animal [the dog that tears and howls . . . that lies within], to have our heart free of him . . . that makes us . . .cry for death.' As in *Me Again*, the first two lines only are then quoted. In *The Holiday*, line 2 reads: 'Shall carve it out. I'll have thy heart, thy life.'

Fallen, Fallen, p. 74
Lucifer is the subject of the poem.

Will Ever?, p. 75
'the crafty hand . . .': cf. Blake's 'Tyger'.

Ceux qui luttent . . ., p. 75
In 'A Turn Outside', *Me Again*, pp. 341–2:
    s.s.: It is on the French proverb that says, 'Those who struggle are those who live'. . . .
    INTERLOCUTOR: Nice to have got some Latin in too.
    s.s.: What? Oh yes, I hadn't noticed that. *I see.*
    INTERLOCUTOR: Ha ha ha.
    s.s.: But this idea you know of struggling being living. Really in a way I suppose it is.

Fuite d'Enfance, p. 76
In *The Holiday*, p. 162: 'This poem makes such a terrible picture of a terrible state of mind.' In *The Holiday* the first two lines have 'friends' not 'loves'.

Cf. Blake's 'Broken love':

> My Spectre around me night and day
> Like a wild beast guards my way;
> My emanation far within
> Weeps incessantly for my sin.

'Fuite d'Enfance': flight of childhood.

'A leur insu. . .': Unknown to them, I have come to make my farewells.

Mother, What Is Man?

Human Affection, p. 77

In 'What Poems are Made Of', *Me Again*, p. 129: 'I see a mother and her child, standing by a greengrocer's stall; they are poor people, poorly clad.'

The Face, p. 79

In 'A Turn Outside', *Me Again*, pp. 346–7:

> s.s.: You know the hymn, 'There is a green hill far away'? Well, I wrote a poem called 'The Face' that goes to that tune. This poem is about *another* person's faults, not my own, so forgive me if it is censorious. But it is probably something he is not entirely to blame for. This person in the poem, had a silver-spoon upbringing and a doting Mama. As well as the deep stupidity he was born with, poor fellow, no doubt it was not easy for him. . . .
>
> INTERLOCUTOR: First Lady T's face, before the looking glass, and now this poor fellow's, and in both of them you are afraid, I think, that it is your own face you see?

If I Lie Down, p. 80

In 'Too Tired for Words', *Me Again*, p. 118: 'The dangerous thoughts of a little child I wrote about. The child stands in his flannel sleeping suit beside his bed and he is saying to himself these two lines.'

She Said . . ., p. 81

Cf. Blake's 'Gnomic Verses' xxi:

> The Angel that presided o'er my birth
> Said, 'Little creature, form'd of joy and mirth,
> Go, love without the help of anything on earth.'

(Included by Stevie Smith in her choice for the *Batsford Book of Children's Verse*.)

Quand on n'a pas ce que l'on aime . . ., p. 81

'Quand on n'a . . .': When one has not got what one loves, one must love what one has. French proverb, in letter from Roger du Bussy-Rabertin to Mme de Sévigny, May 23, 1667.

'O Death in Life': cf. Tennyson, *The Princess*, IV, lines 39–40, 'Deep as first love, and wild with all regret;/O Death in Life, the days that are no more.'

Distractions and the Human Crowd, p. 82

'following the tea-parties,/(And the innumerable conferences...)': a faint and uncharacteristic echo of Eliot, 'The Love Song of J. Alfred Prufrock' ('after tea and cakes and ices') and 'Four Quartets' ('Here is a place of disaffection').

My Heart was Full, p. 84

In 'Simply Living' (1964), *Me Again*, p. 108: 'I wrote this poem, accompanied by a drawing of a little creature swinging on his stomach on a swing, to show the enjoyment that lurks in simplicity.' (She goes on to say that the writer John Cowper Powys knows all about this simplicity: cf. *The Holiday*, p. 124, 'It is . . . Powys who has this fullest free feeling of the pleasures of *instinctuality*.')

Croft, p. 84

In 'Simply Living' (1964), *Me Again*, p. 108, this follows on from 'My Heart was Full': 'They will probably write off the simple ones, as they wrote off poor Croft.'

In 'Too Tired for Words' (1956), *Me Again*, p. 115: '"He is soft" may be *their* point of view about it, but it is not ours.'

Rencontres Funestes, p. 85

'Rencontres Funestes': fatal, or deadly, encounters.

In 'What Poems are Made Of', *Me Again*, p. 127: 'I like to walk across Hyde Park where the loving couples lie.'

The Repentance of Lady T, p. 85

See note to 'The Face' (p. 79).

In 'A Turn Outside', *Me Again*, p. 341: 'A lot of these sung poems go to church tunes and they stem from the liturgy as well as from *Hymns Ancient and Modern*. But I think this is all right, don't you?—for the poems that have a religious theme . . . like this one.' Her reading of this poem (BBC recording 10 June 1963) 'goes to a sort of tune'.

The Magic Morning, p. 86

'the mauve sedge': cf. 'The sedge is withered from the lake/And no birds sing', Keats, 'La Belle Dame Sans Merci'.

'nervy bold and grim': cf. *The Holiday*, p. 192, 'Uncle I am nervy bold and grim.'

'mise-en-scène': theatrical production, staging.

Old Ghosts, p. 88
'By one half as much power as the Roman Centurion': see De Quincey, *Confessions of An English Opium Eater*, Part III, 'The Pains of Opium', 'Many children have the power of painting, as it were, upon the darkness all sorts of phantoms . . . as a child once said to me . . . "I can tell them to go, and they go; but sometimes they come when I don't tell them to come." He had by one-half as unlimited a command over apparitions as a Roman centurion over his soldiers. In the middle of 1817 this faculty became increasingly distressing to me. . . .' Stevie Smith can tell her ghosts to come, but not to go.

The Failed Spirit, p. 89
In 'Too Tired for Words', *Me Again*, p. 115: 'In the war I thought lonely people became happier, but in myself I condemned it.'
'adamantine': hard, unbreakable. Cf. Milton, *Paradise Lost*, I, 44, 'In adamantine chains and penal fire'.

The Recluse, p. 89
'My soul . . .': cf. Tennyson's 'Song' ('A spirit haunts the year's last hours'), 'My very heart faints and my whole soul grieves/At the moist rich smell of the rotting leaves.' Cf. also 'The Poet's Mind' (a poem much liked by Stevie Smith and included in the *Batsford Book of Children's Verse*): 'There is frost in your breath/Which would blight the plants.'
'Pashy': cf. Browning's *Childe Roland*, ''Tis a brute must walk/Pashing their life out, with a brute's intent.'

Torquemada, p. 90
See note to 'The Church' (p. 40).

The Story of a Story, p. 91

(*Me Again*, pp. 50–9.)
Introduction to *Me Again*, p. 4: 'Margery Hemming, in her copy of "The Story of a Story", wrote a key to the identity of its characters: Stevie . . . is the writer Helen, Margery Hemming and her husband Francis (eminent civil servant and lepidopterist) are the couple, Roland and Bella; Ba is the art historian, Phoebe Pool; and Lopez is the writer, Inez Holden. The story . . . in "The Story of a Story" is "Sunday at Home".'
   Letter to Kay Dick, 12 February 1946, *Me Again*, p. 289: 'I think one could write a wonderful tale about a group of coterie friends writing about each other and the zig-zagging antics they would get up to to foil the litigious. . . .'
'It is the moment to look at a horse': cf. the numerous times in which Stevie Smith prefers animals to humans. Walt Whitman's 'I think I could

turn and live with animals', from 'Song of Myself', is included in her choice for the *Batsford Book of Children's Verse*.

'the ferocious messages': the messenger speech from the *Bacchae*, cf. p. 37.

Q.C.: Queen's Counsel.

Von Hügel: (1852–1926). Roman Catholic religious writer.

'She was a Christian of the neo-Platonic school': cf. *Novel on Yellow Paper*, p. 176, 'It is no further than the neo-platonic idea of Christ that I can come.'

'time to pray': cf. Cynthia's prayers in 'The House of Over-Dew' (p. 177).

'The third hour's . . .': Richard Crashaw, 'The Office of the Holy Cross', *Sacred Poems* (1648). Also quoted in *Over the Frontier*, p. 69.

'Come, peace of God, et cetera': The communion service, 'The peace of God, which passeth all understanding, be amongst you and remain with you always.'

Elsheimer: Adam Elsheimer (1578–1610). German landscape painter who worked in Italy; very precise small works done on copper with careful attention to effects of light.

Grünewald: Mathis Grünewald (1470/80–1528). German religious painter. His altar of Isenheim is a painted counterpart to Dante's *Divine Comedy*.

'Spiritual things are spiritually discerned': The dream-girl's book is an anthology of Pauline and neo-Platonic thought. The first sentence is based on Paul, I Corinthians: 2, 14. The third ('Let those be silent', etc.) is from Plotinus, *Ennead*, I, 6 ('On Beauty'), iv. The ideas are drawn from Plotinus and from Dionysius the Areopagite (esp. *De divinis Nominibus*, I).

'Syler's Green', p. 100

(*Me Again*, pp. 84ff.)

'Syler's Green': i.e., Palmers Green.

'that is how one is apt to remember past times': cf. 'Archie and Tina' (p. 175).

'there in the green depths of Scapelands Lake': cf. Kay Dick, *Ivy and Stevie*, pp. 52–3, 'Grovelands Park . . . at Southgate . . . (still has) a huge lake, which is the source of inspiration for a great many of my deep country poems about lakes and people getting bewitched, enchanted, *ensorcellé*.'

Grendel: Grendel is the name of the monster killed by Beowulf in the Anglo-Saxon poem. The hero then has to kill Grendel's mother in her lair under the water.

Childhood and Interruption, p. 101

(*Me Again*, p. 234. Undated.)

Cf. Blake's 'The Echoing Green'.

The Holiday

'The Christian solution', p. 102
(*The Holiday*, pp. 42–3.)
Tom: Celia's cousin Tom Fox, who has been mentally ill, and with whose father, Heber, a vicar, (from whom Tom is estranged) Celia goes to stay in *The Holiday*.
Grey Eminence: Biography of Cardinal Richelieu by Aldous Huxley (1941).
Father D'Arcy: Father Martin Cyril D'Arcy (b. 1888). Jesuit philosophical theologian, author of *The Nature of Belief* (1931), *Belief and Reason* (1944), *The Mind and Heart of Love* (1945), etc.
The Screwtape Letters: (1942), a work on Christianity (in the form of an exchange of letters) by C. S. Lewis (1898–1963).
    Cf. 'Sunday at Home' (1949), *Me Again*, p. 47: 'There is something frightening about the Christian idea. . . . The plodding on and on . . . the de-moting and the up-grading; the marks and the punishments and the smugness . . . like school.'
    Cf. 'Too Tired for Words' (1956), *Me Again*, p. 112: 'If one is tired all the time I do not see how one can accept the Christian religion that is so exhausting and neat, and tied up neatly for all eternity with rewards and punishments and plodding on (that too much bears the mark of our humanity with its intolerable urge to boss, confine and intimidate).'

'The post-war', p. 104

(*The Holiday*, p. 90.)
'Caz', or Casmilus, takes the name given to the heroine of *Novel on Yellow Paper* and *Over the Frontier*. Pompey becomes Celia. Celia loves her cousin Caz, but an old family rumour—that they may be brother and sister—comes between them.
'the post-war': see Kay Dick, *Ivy and Stevie*, p. 47, 'It's just after the war. I wrote it actually during the war and I couldn't get it published . . . I kept on putting in things that were after the war, like the troubles in Palestine, and it was in such a muddle that I had to call it the after-the-war period.'
In spite of this, the political analysis of England is extremely cogent and forceful.

'Voices against England in the Night', p. 105
(*The Holiday*, pp. 127–8.)
The context is a difficult conversation in which Celia is trying to defend British policy in India. Throughout *The Holiday*, her poems are incorporated into the narrative. In *Collected Poems*, the first three stanzas are in inverted commas, making it clear that this is the voice of Goebbels (the Nazi minister of propaganda, 1933–1945). In *Collected Poems*, line 5

reads: 'And the songs you sing are the songs you sung'; line 6 reads: 'On a braver day . . .'; the last line reads: '. . . O history turn thy pages fast!'

Stevie Smith opposes the pacifists and those who say that the empire is outworn.

Cf. the earlier accounts of Germany in *Novel on Yellow Paper* and *Over the Frontier*.

'This writing business', p. 106
(*The Holiday*, pp. 156–8.)
'Tom Snooks': cf. 'Tom Snooks the Pundit' (p. 168).
'too set up': cf. letter to John Hayward, 31 August 194?, *Me Again*, p. 286, 'I am not *sure* that it is an absolutely good thing that the prizes of writing are so enormous, it is the one form of art that is overpraised in England, if I were drawing a Muse of Writing (I forget which one it is) I should dress her in gold cloth and give her a cocktail in her hand.'
Wilberforce: (1759–1833). Politician and philanthropist who abolished the British slave trade.
Newton: (1643–1727). English mathematician, physicist, astronomer, discovered law of gravity.
Harley: (1661–1724). British statesman, negotiated treaty of Utrecht, 1713.
Coulton: George Coulton (1858–1957). Author of *Five Centuries of Religion* (1923 *et seq.*), *Life in the Middle Ages* (1928–9), etc.

'Everything is in fits and splinters', p. 109
(*The Holiday*, pp. 142–3.)
'the Proverbs': of Solomon, e.g. 'Go to the ant, thou sluggard; consider her ways, and be wise.'
Polonius: speech of advice to Laertes ('Neither a borrower nor a lender be . . .'), *Hamlet*, I, iii, 75.
Lopez: see 'The Story of a Story' (p. 91) and note. Lopez (Inez Holden) is also in *Novel on Yellow Paper*.
'Prenatally biassed . . .': see 'Breughel' (p. 55) and note.

The Royal Dane, p. 109
In *The Holiday*, p. 190: 'It is Hamlet's father's ghost's farewell to Hamlet. . . . I sing it to the tune of Sullivan's "Of that there is no shadow of doubt, no possible probable shadow of doubt."' This is greeted with '"Ha ha ha. Tee hee. . . . It's 'sulphurous'," said Caz, wiping his eyes.'
Also in *Me Again*, p. 223.

Harold's Leap

The Castle, p. 110
In *The Holiday*, pp. 174–5: 'This poem is not sensible, it is, perhaps you

will say, morally indefensible. . . . [After reading two stanzas] I began to sigh more deeply as I read on in my poem, for the hopelessness of the situation and the lack of what is sensible.'

In 'A Turn Outside', *Me Again*, p. 339: 'It is deliciously happy, it is quite radiant, but of course it is a fairy story, it is the East of the Sun and West of the Moon, Cupid–Psyche story, really I am afraid that is what it is.' (She tells her 'Interlocutor', who is Death: 'You like it because it is out of the world.')

Harold's Leap, p. 111
In a Broadcast to Schools (BBC recording 8 June 1966) she says: '[This] is the very opposite of "The Weak Monk". Unlike him, Harold is very brave indeed. He never tired of trying tasks that a conceited man would have avoided through fear of failure, or a timid man because he was timid. Not so Harold. He believed, as Browning said, that "a man's reach should exceed his grasp/Or what's a heaven for?" ['Andrea del Sarto', lines 97–8.] I like Harold very much, he died doing more than he was able.'

Touch and Go, p. 112
In *The Holiday*, p. 71, in the context of a discussion of England's treatment of its colonies: 'things may be changing'.

In *The Holiday*, verse 2, line 2 reads: 'He is bowed by sorrow and fret'; verse 6, line 1 reads: 'Oh the delicate creature' and verse 7, line 1 reads: 'Look he moves—that is more than a prayer'.

Man is a Spirit, p. 113
There is a play on guest/ghost, and on 'host' as meaning, also, the Eucharist.

The River God, p. 113
Subtitle not in *Collected Poems*. *CP* has 'smooth' for 'smoothe'.

When reading this poem (BBC recording 29 March 1956) Stevie Smith comments on the river god's attempt to live with the lady: 'It was not, I need hardly say, much good.'

The Ambassador, p. 114
Subtitle not in *Collected Poems*.
See note to 'A visitor' (p. 41) and 'Casmilus' (p. 60). Stevie Smith has mixed Janus and Mercury together.
Lemprière: author of the standard Classical Dictionary.

Stevie Smith comments (BBC recording 8 June 1966): 'A riddle poem . . . about a very subtle and powerful god.'

Persephone, p. 114
The story of Persephone and Demeter is told in the 2nd Homeric Hymn.

Persephone, ravished by Pluto, King of the Underworld, is sought for by her mother Demeter, who is allowed to have her back on condition that she spends six months of every year in Hades. (The seasonal myth is similar to the story of Isis and Osiris.) The story has been retold by Goethe, Schiller, Milton (whose lines Celia quotes in *The Holiday*, p. 150); Shelley ('Song of Proserpine'); Tennyson ('Demeter and Persephone'); Swinburne ('Hymn to Persephone' and 'Garden of Persephone') and Graves.

In *The Holiday*, pp. 149–51, Celia is riding with Caz; their dialogue is given in 'A Turn Outside' to Stevie Smith and the Interlocutor, who turns out to be Death. Elsewhere Stevie Smith refers to *The Holiday* as 'Married to Death' (*Me Again*, p. 263) and 'Death and the Girl' (*Me Again*, p. 287), and in 'Is There Life Before the Grave?' (1947) (*Me Again*, pp. 60–73), scenes from *The Holiday* are given as though taking place after death. It is clear from this that Stevie Smith identifies Celia and Caz with Persephone and Pluto. In their ride together, Celia asks Caz: 'Do you like Death?' She is reminded by the scenery of the legend in the *Iliad* that the shades must have blood to drink before they can speak. (Also referred to in 'A Dream of Nourishment', *Collected Poems*, p. 344, and 'A Turn Outside'.)

In her Broadcast for Schools (BBC recording 8 June 1966) she calls it 'Persephone in Winter' and says: 'I have made Persephone a girl who loves winter and snow and a curious light you get in winter.... Persephone even likes the dark places which can be frightening.... Another thread is what Persephone feels about her mother. She doesn't want to be sought for all the time.'

Do Take Muriel Out, p. 115
In 'A Turn Outside', *Me Again*, pp. 344–5:
    INTERLOCUTOR: ... that last dance cheers me up. Over the Brocken? In the Hartz Mountains, perhaps? But Muriel's fate—fate is not very happy?
    S.S.: Oh, I don't know. Her values were wrong, now perhaps they will be put right ... yes, there is the German feeling, I cannot think why, I have no very fond feeling for Germany. All the same there is something of the Gretchen song in it ... 'My heart is heavy, my peace is gone, I shall find it never, O never again.'
'the blasted heath': *Macbeth*, I, iii, 77.

Muriel's story is another version of 'Death and the girl'. Stevie Smith was fond of Edgar Allan Poe's poem on this theme, 'Annabel Lee' (included in her choice for the *Batsford Book of Children's Verse*).
Collected Poems has 'have' in line 4.

The Weak Monk, p. 116
In Broadcast for Schools (BBC recording 8 June 1966) Stevie Smith compares the weak monk to 'the sort of thing a timid writer might do but

he should not'. One must try to get one's work published; one only 'hoards' out of 'vanity or fear of criticism' (or 'fear of religious censorship' in the monk's case).

Le Singe Qui Swing, p. 117
In *The Holiday*, p. 99, Celia remembers her childhood in India: 'And I remember there was an ape that went with the house. And we children ... used to watch him as he swung, swinging at midnight in the moonlight. . . . This ape that went with the house was called Sinbad, he was already an old animal. . . . Believe me, Reader, that animal was happy in a quiet way, swinging at his own sweet will in the warm Southern night and the mellow moonbeam.'

This is a good example of how poem, picture, and tune are combined.

Cf. 'My Heart was Full' (p. 84) and note.

'Duty was his Lodestar', p. 119
In 'Too Tired for Words' (1956), *Me Again*, p. 111: 'this one with its tired reading of Lobster for Lodestar'.

Cf. Lewis Carroll: Alice's misrenderings of well-known poems by, e.g. Isaac Watts, 'How doth the little crocodile/Improve his shining tail', etc.

In 'A Turn Outside', *Me Again*, p. 338: 'This poem turns on duty. You see the child has been told that duty is one's lodestar. But she is rebellious, this child, she will have none of it, so she says lobster instead of lodestar, and so makes a mock of it, and makes a monkey of the kind schoolteacher (that was all the time thinking only of Harrow and "Forty Years On", that my school had a very special devotion to. . .).'

The After-thought, p. 119
In the story in Grimm, Rapunzel in her tower lets down her hair to the prince, but the witch who is keeping her captive overhears them, cuts off Rapunzel's hair, and blinds the prince. In the end Rapunzel, wandering through the world, finds the prince, and her tears restore his sight.
Edgar Allan Poe: this is a reference to 'The Purloined Letter'.
Titurel: a legendary knight who guarded the Holy Grail. See note to 'In My Dreams' (p. 72).

In reading this poem (BBC recording 10 June 1963) Stevie Smith comments: 'A love poem that is also a literary situation because the young man is always thinking about something else.'

The Deserter, p. 120
In 'Too Tired for Words' (1956), *Me Again*, pp. 113–14: 'Of course there's another thing tiredness can do (and this is always so welcome)—it can provide an excuse for not writing at all. One hugs one's disabilities, one cultivates them, one becomes—like the wretch I have put in the next poem—a deserter to ill health. (The wretch was a writer but now he lies

in his hospital bed—and let the Muse go hang.)' *Collected Poems* has 'But they all admit I shall' in line 4 and 'I shall keep' in line 8.

A Humane Materialist..., p. 120
In *The Holiday*, pp. 191–2: 'This humane person, this old-fashioned Trotskyite piece, is standing in the front row, he can smell the burning flesh of the heretic. This heretic has been very much tortured, because you see his deviationist opinions are not very clear cut, so you see, poor fellow, he has not been able to frame a confession that will fit in with what the torturers want, always what he says is not quite, as the editors say, "what we had in mind".... So in the end it is no good, both sides give up, he is "an unrepentant heretic" ... so what is left of him is now being burnt. So this humane materialist is standing in the front row. This is what he says, it is the poem.'

Mr Over, p. 121
In 'A Turn Outside', *Me Again*, p. 350: 'A non-activiste, a broody egg-head, say, is standing by the grave of a brave soldier who died fighting. The egg-head would like to die too, but knowing that he has always been so feeble, so un-brave and so un-fighting, not to say plum languid, he fears for his reception on the other side....'

Our Bog is Dood, p. 121
Cf. Wordsworth's 'We Are Seven' (''Twas throwing words away; for still/The little maid would have her will,/And said, "Nay, we are seven!"').
Metre: cf. Lewis Carroll's 'The Walrus and the Carpenter' ('But answer came there none/ And this was scarcely odd, because/They'd eaten every one') or 'The White Knight's Song' ('Come, tell me how you live, I cried,/And what it is you do!').
'within each infant eye': cf. Blake's 'London', 'In every infant's cry of fear'.

Who Shot Eugenie?, p. 123
This is a version of the plot of *Over the Frontier*, in which Pompey's fantastical wartime journey makes her think about the effects of power. In the novel and the poem the journey is reminiscent of Browning's *Childe Roland to the Dark Tower Came*, which Stevie Smith frequently refers to (see 'The Fugitive's Ride', *Collected Poems*, p. 79; 'Childe Rolandine', *Collected Poems*, p. 331; 'Brickenden, Hertfordshire, *Collected Poems*, p. 114; and 'The Recluse' (p. 89)). In 'A Very Pleasant Evening' (1946), *Me Again*, pp. 33–4, Childe Roland is said to be 'an exact spiritual description of the detail of the Flanders battlefield'. In 'At School', *Me Again*, p. 119, she refers to it as one of her favourite childhood poems. Pompey's

journey in *Over the Frontier* closely evokes *Childe Roland* (lines 226–7, 244). Verse 4 of this poem ('Why is it starlight...') is quoted in *Over the Frontier*, p. 244, in the course of the journey, after this passage: 'Starlight has always had an effect of the uneasy upon my mind, so cold, so distant, unfreundlich, so remote. It disturbs and excites me, calling to everything that is in me of the inhuman, the disembodied, the separate....'

'I said no word': cf. 'Nor We Of Her To Him' (p. 174).

Not Waving but Drowning

Not Waving but Drowning, p. 128
In 'Too Tired for Words', *Me Again*, p. 113: 'It's a tightrope business, this pulling oneself together, and can give rise to misunderstandings which may prove fatal, as in this poem I wrote about a poor fellow who got drowned.'

The Blue from Heaven, p. 129
For the legends of King Arthur, see Malory's *Le Morte D'Arthur*, and Tennyson's *Idylls of the King*.

A Dream of Comparison, p. 131
In *The Holiday*, p. 199: 'Uncle, I cry, I detest your Christianity that will be so positive. Unknown, unknown, unknown, let that be the life to come and the world that lies beyond. Uncle, if I were the Virgin Mary, I would say: No, no, I will have no part in it, no saviour, no world to come, nothing.'

In 'Too Tired for Words', *Me Again*, p. 117: 'Milton puts a very curious anti-life argument into Eve's mouth. Eve says in effect (they have just been expelled from the Garden of Eden) "If all our children are to be condemned to discomfort in this life and the probability of eternal torment in the life to come, would it not be better not to have any children?" It is interesting to compare Eve's attitude (or Milton's rather, but of course he quickly pulled himself together, drawing back the delicate toe from the swamp of heresy) with the brave *"fiat mihi"* ["Behold the handmaid of the Lord, be it unto me according to thy word"] of the Virgin Mary, the fiery authoress of the Magnificat.'

Paradise Lost, Book X:

> Childless thou art, childless remain:
> So death shall be deceived his glut, and with us two
> Be forced to satisfy his ravenous maw....
>
> Let us seek Death, or he not found, supply
> With our own hands his office on ourselves;
> Why stand we longer shivering under fears,

That show no end but Death, and have the power,
Of many ways to die the shortest choosing,
Destruction with destruction to destroy.
                                      (lines 989–91, 1001–6)

My Hat, p. 132
'It is always early morning . . .': cf. Tennyson's 'The Lotos-Eaters', 'A land/In which it seemed always afternoon'.

Anger's Freeing Power, p. 133
The Raven suggests Edgar Allan Poe, (and 'The Three Ravens' is in Stevie Smith's selection for the *Batsford Book of Children's Verse*), but the idea is Blakean ('Damn braces; Bless relaxes', *Proverbs of Hell*).

Fafnir and the Knights, p. 134
Fafnir: in the Norse myth, the Volsungsaga, Fafnir is the son of Hreidmar, whom he kills for a cursed treasure. He is turned into a dragon and killed by Sigurd. In Wagner's *Siegfried*, Fafnir is a giant changed into a dragon who guards the Nibelung treasure and is slain by Siegfried.

Songe D'Athalie, p. 135
From Racine's *Athalie*, II, v, 487–506:

> Un songe (me devrais-je inquiéter d'un songe?)
> Entretient dans mon coeur un chagrin qui le ronge.
> Je l'évite partout, partout il me poursuit.
> C'était pendant l'horreur d'une profonde nuit.
> Ma mère Jézabel devant moi s'est montrée,
> Comme au jour de sa mort pompeusement parée.
> Ses malheurs n'avaient point abattu sa fierté;
> Même elle avait encor cet éclat emprunté
> Dont elle eut soin de peindre et d'orner son visage,
> Pour réparer des ans l'irréparable outrage.
> 'Tremble,' m'a-t-elle dit, 'fille digne de moi.
> Le cruel Dieu des Juifs l'emporte aussi sur toi.
> Je te plains de tomber dans ses mains redoutables,
> Ma fille.' En achevant ces mots épouvantables,
> Son ombre vers mon lit a paru se baisser;
> Et moi, je lui tendais les mains pour l'embrasser.
> Mais je n'ai plus trouvé qu'un horrible mélange
> D'os et de chair meurtris, et traînés dans la fange,
> Des lambeaux pleins de sang, et des membres affreux
> Que des chiens dévorants se disputaient entre eux.

The Hostage, p. 136
'Even as a child . . .': cf. 'Infant' (p. 45), and *Novel on Yellow Paper*.

Dido's Farewell to Aeneas, p. 138
From Virgil, *Aeneid*, IV, 638–72.
Translated by W. F. Jackson Knight (Penguin Classics, 1956):
'I have lived my life and finished the course which Fortune allotted me. Now my wraith shall pass in state to the world below. I have established a noble city. I have lived to see my own ramparts built. I have avenged my husband and punished the brother who was our foe. Happy, all too happy, should I have been, if only the Dardan ships had never reached my coast!' With this cry she buried her face in the bed and continued: 'I shall die, and die unavenged; but die I shall. Yes, yes; this is the way I like to go into the dark.'
'our Dardanian sailor': Aeneas was a descendant of Dardanus, who founded the kingdom of Troy.
'my abominable brother': Dido's brother Pygmalion killed her husband, Sichaeus, and became king of Tyre. Dido revenged herself on her brother and founded Carthage.

Away, Melancholy, p. 138
Cf. Milton, *L'Allegro*: 'Hence, loathed melancholy...'
'The ant is busy': cf. 'Everything is in fits and splinters' (p. 109) and note.
'Man aspires/To good': cf. 'Touch and Go' (p. 112) and 'Was He Married?' (p. 154).

The Jungle Husband, p. 140
Reading this poem (BBC recording 10 June 1963) Stevie Smith comments: 'It is not a happy situation ... he is rather drunk.' She reads it in a 'drunken' voice.
'anacondas': large South American snakes.

I Remember, p. 140
In a letter to Sally Chilver, 20 November 1956, *Me Again*, p. 303, Stevie Smith describes this as one of 'my new ones ... [in which] I have a boss shot at a general feeling of warmth & affection'. Reading this poem (BBC recording 10 June 1963) she describes it as 'a happy love poem'.

God the Eater, p. 141
In 'Too Tired for Words', *Me Again*, p. 116: 'To live all one's life with no great feeling for life ... invites life's revenge.... All the writer can do then is to offer his life, which seems to him so shadowy and inconsiderable, to some god or other for him to chew upon and make the best of.'
In *The Holiday*, p. 200: 'But close within there sits the soul ... that feeds upon the tears and the blood. And why should it not so feed? Is it not of

God? sent out to be lost for a time? to return? So let it feed and grow fat, and return to God in admirable plight, yes, let it feed.'

Reading this poem (BBC recording 29 March 1956) she says it is about 'a human being who is in a religious predicament . . . he loves but he cannot believe . . . for him God is an eater and so he offers him his life to eat'.

The Airy Christ, p. 141

E. V. Rieu's translation of *The Four Gospels* was published in 1952.

Cf. 'The Story of a Story' (p. 91), her feeling that she is 'a Christian of the neo-Platonic school' who can imagine Christ in triumph but not on the cross. The idea that Christ's original teaching and character have been travestied by the 'working laws' of the Christian church is found in Blake ('The Everlasting Gospel'; 'A Memorable Fancy' in *The Marriage of Heaven and Hell*) and Emerson.
Metre: 8-stress trochaic tetrameter, cf. Tennyson's 'Locksley Hall'.
Collected Poems has 'splendour' in line 1.

Dear Little Sirmio, p. 142
Catullus' Poem xxxi:

> Paene insularum, Sirmio, insularumque
> Ocelle . . . O quid solutis est beatius curis?
> Cum mens onus reponit, ac peregrino
> Labore fessi venimus larem ad nostrum,
> Desideratoque acquiescimus lecto.
> Hoc est quod unum est pro laboribus tantis.
> Salve O venusta Sirmio atque hero gaude;
> Gaudete vosque O Lydiae lacus undae;
> Ridete quidquid est domi cachinnorum.

> What joy is like it? to be quit of care
> And drop my load, and after weary miles
> Come home, and sink upon the bed that so
> I used to dream of: this one thing is worth
> All that long service. Hail, sweet Sirmio!
> Welcome thy lord with laughter, and give back
> Your laughter, waters of the Lydian lake:
> Laugh, home of mine, with all your maddest mirth.

Tennyson's 'Frater Ave atque Vale' combines two poems by Catullus, this one to Sirmio and the farewell to his dead brother. See also Tennyson's 'Hendecasyllabics', 'All composed in a metre of Catullus', and cf. 'Hendecasyllables' (p. 182).

'Great Unaffected Vampires and the Moon', p. 143
In 'Cats in Colour' (1959), *Me Again*, p. 145, she says that the cats in this poem 'set the ghostly scene'. This landscape has been influenced by

Grovelands Park (see 'Syler's Green' p. 100, note) and by *Childe Roland*.
Metre: iambic pentameter with final alexandrine.

At School, p. 144
Paolo and Francesca: The story is told in Dante's *Inferno*, Canto V.
Francesca was married to Giovanni Malatesta; her guilty love for his
younger brother Paolo was discovered and they were both put to death
in about 1289.

In 'At School' (1960), *Me Again*, pp. 121–4: 'It is a story-poem, a
ghost-story poem, of two children who loved each other and are now at
school. Yes, but they are not quite children and it is not quite school they
are at. (The sub-title tells you that at once.) It is the girl who does most of
the talking, she is absolutely idiotic. . . . The children in the poem are
young, loving and sad. . . . They do not understand yet about the school
they are at. It is a sort of Purgatory, a school where they have to learn to
be better and wiser and "older". Already, though they do not know it,
they are making progress, because even the little goose of a girl can say
"They do not mind if we are not very bright." But this school is a bit of a
forcing ground too, with the harsh lights, and the radiators turned full
on. And the shadows are not friendly. And when they ride out together,
it is a melancholy landscape, and where they think they would like to go
. . . the "sea-pool" . . . is never quite near enough for the time they have.
It is an ominous place, running up close to panic. But learn they must.
And the skies above them are ominous, with a hint of barbed bayonets,
grown rusty. . . . Those who teach them are "patient". And one knows it
will take a long time. The idea is also this: that human affections and
passions, likes and dislikes, are "young" . . . and that all this must be
burnt away, taught and learnt away, before the children can "grow up".
But what are they supposed to grow up into? Ah, that is a
mystery—something that seems cold to us, cold with more than the
touch of death.'

Reading it in a Broadcast for Schools (BBC recording 8 June 1966) she
says there was something in it of her own school, but 'you know poets
pick what they want from innumerable sources and memories . . . it isn't
important'.
Collected Poems has 'really always' in line 11, 'me' in line 23 and 'come' in
line 24.

The Old Sweet Dove of Wiveton, p. 146
In Kay Dick, *Ivy and Stevie*, p. 37: 'I do adore [this poem] so because my
Norfolk holidays come into it.'
''Twas the voice . . .': cf. Lewis Carroll, *Alice's Adventures in Wonderland*,
''Tis the voice of the Lobster: I heard him declare/You have baked me too
brown, I must sugar my hair' (from Isaac Watts, ''Tis the voice of the
sluggard').

My Heart Goes Out, p. 147
Cf. 'God the Eater' (p. 141).
    See 'What Poems are Made Of' (1969), p. 168. That passage is followed
by this poem.
    In a letter to Sally Chilver, 20 November 1956, *Me Again*, p. 303: 'What I
like about this is that it's so *apt* to be "my creator-in-law".'
    In 'A Turn Outside', *Me Again*, pp. 356–7: 'I would rather have *nox est
perpetua una dormienda* [Catullus], I would rather have Lucretius, "Where
we are Death is not and where Death is we cannot be." An eternal sleep,
Nothing, an End. That makes me happy, then I can say what I said in this
poem.'

Magna est Veritas, p. 148
'Magna est veritas et praevalet': 1 Esdras 4:41, *Apocrypha*. Quoted by
Thomas Brooks, 'The Crown and Glory of Christianity' (1662): 'For
(magna est veritas et praevalebit) great is truth, and shall prevail.'

Farewell, p. 149
'Farewell dear world/With the waters around you curled': cf. W. B.
Rands, 'The World':
                Great, wide, beautiful, wonderful world,
                With the wonderful water round you curled,
                And the wonderful grass upon your breast——
                World, you are beautifully drest.

'Cats in Colour', p. 150

(*Me Again*, pp. 139–40.)
Fullers: a tea-shop chain.

'My Muse', p. 151

(*Me Again*, p. 126.) (Stevie Smith quotes 'The Ambassador' after 'this
animal is dangerous'.)
Peleus: the only mortal to marry an immortal, Thetis, a sea-goddess who
turned herself into different shapes to try and escape him. Their
offspring was Achilles.
Gavin Bone: author of *Beowulf in Modern Verse* (1945), *Anglo-Saxon Poetry*
(1943) and *Tindale and the English Language* (1938).

Selected Poems

Thoughts about the Person from Porlock, p. 152
Coleridge, Preliminary Note to 'Kubla Khan': 'On awaking he ...

instantly and eagerly wrote down the lines that are here preserved. At this moment he was unfortunately called out by a person on business from Porlock.'
Porson: there was a poet called Porson (1759–1808) who wrote very bad epigrams.
'Warlock': sorcerer.
'the One Above who is experimenting': cf. 'God and the Devil' (p. 46).

Thoughts about the Christian Doctrine of Eternal Hell, p. 154
Cf. 'Some Impediments to Christian Commitment' (1968), *Me Again*, p. 155: 'I read my bible and I saw that the lofty Christ believed, too, and taught this monstrous doctrine of eternal hell. . . . The doctrine of hell, so surely based upon Christ's own words, became for me the first Fault. . . .'

Was He Married?, p. 154
In 'Some Impediments to Christian Commitment', *Me Again*, p. 162: 'It is a poem for two voices. One voice, the simple, young one, is complaining that Christ could not have known human suffering because human suffering has its roots in imperfection, and he was perfect. The other voice is older, and not very kind.'
     Reading this poem (BBC recording 10 June 1963) she says 'there is a fierce fire of argument in the poem', and distinguishes very emphatically between the two voices.

My Muse, p. 157
First four lines in 'Too Tired for Words' (1956), *Me Again*, p. 111: 'The Muse complains endlessly; or, feeling guilty, one complains on her behalf.'
     Second half in 'My Muse' (1960), *Me Again*, p. 125: 'She is always howling into an indifferent ear.'
     Cf. 'Who is This Who Howls and Mutters?' (p. 147).

The Frog Prince

The Frog Prince, p. 158
Story taken from the Brothers Grimm.
     Reading this poem (BBC recording 10 June 1963) she comments: 'The Frog Prince has this feeling of hope in death.'

Phèdre, p. 160
See *Novel on Yellow Paper*, p. 129: 'Look at Euripides' *Hippolytus*, and now look at Racine's *Phèdre*. It is the same story . . . but Euripides is very profoundly unquiet and restless, so that it disturbs the tragedy, but Racine is very serene, very severe, very austere and simple, and the

tragedy very strong and not broken up at all, but very strong and simple. . . . This is Greek. This is truly Greek, and what the Greek is.'

Phaedra, wife of Theseus and stepmother of Hippolytus, tells Hippolytus of her love. He rejects her and she falsely accuses him of having tried to rape her. Theseus begs Neptune to punish Hippolytus, and he is killed by a sea-monster. Phaedra confesses and kills herself. In Racine, Aricie is Hippolytus' beloved.

'I wonder why Proust . . .': 'Combray', *Swann's Way*, Vol. I, p. 120 (trans. Scott Moncrieff), 'Racine did . . . compose a line which is not only fairly rhythmical, but has also what is in my eyes the supreme merit of meaning absolutely nothing . . . "La fille de Minos et de Pasiphaé".' But Stevie Smith is inaccurate here. Bloch, who is pretentious and mannered, is talking to Marcel (who is at this point rather naïve) and Bloch is *praising* Racine for writing a meaningless line. He does not quote both lines.

'Ariadne auf Naxos': Ariadne, Phaedra's sister, helped Theseus to kill the Minotaur and was later abandoned by him on the island of Naxos. Stevie Smith calls her by the title of Strauss's opera.

Pasiphaë: wife of Minos, had an unnatural love for a bull; their offspring was the Minotaur, confined in the labyrinth by Minos to devour the young men and women sent as a yearly tribute to Crete.

Minos: grandfather of the King Minos who was Phaedra's father. He became the supreme judge of the dead.

Animula, vagula, blandula, p. 164

Hadrian's address to his soul, when dying:

> Animula vagula blandula,
> Hospes comesque corporis,
> Quae nunc abibis in loca
> Pallidula rigida nudula,
> Nec ut soles dabis iocos!

'Little soul, wandering, pleasant, guest and companion of the body, into what places wilt thou now go, pale, stiff, naked, nor wilt thou play any longer as thou art wont.' (Duff, *Minor Latin Poems* (Loeb, 1934).)

In *Novel on Yellow Paper*, p. 204, Stevie Smith calls herself 'an *animula, vagula, blandula*, of the office'.

Collected Poems has 'friend and guest' in line 2.

I love . . ., p. 165

'Hooker's green': presumably a reference to the many coloured plates of botanical illustrations in *Exotic Flora*, *British Flora*, and other works by William Jackson Hooker (1785–1865), director of the Royal Botanical Gardens at Kew from 1841.

gamboge: yellow gum resin from Cambodia used as pigment.

magenta: pinky red.

Nodding, p. 166

In 'Cats in Colour' (1959), *Me Again*, p. 136: 'I had a cat once called Tizdal, just such a kitchen fat cat as I love. I wrote this poem about Tizdal, to show the love one can have for an animal, the love that likes to hug and stroke and tickle—and pinch lightly on the sly too, half-mocking. . . . I called it "Nodding"; you'll have had this mood often yourself.'

Voice from the Tomb, p. 167

In 'A Turn Outside', *Me Again*, pp. 335–6:

> s.s.: This one . . . could go either to 'Greenland's Icy Mountains' or 'Jerusalem the Golden'. . . . Did you ever notice by the way what a lot of . . . Macauley's 'Horatius' goes to 'Greenland's Icy Mountains'? [She sings the poem.]
> INTERLOCUTOR: It's a bit of a fiddle, that last line . . . so–o wa–as lost.
> s.s.: Well, it brings the desperateness out.

'What Poems are Made Of', p. 168

(*Me Again*, pp. 127–9.)
'Colour . . .': cf. 'Oh grateful colours, bright looks!' (p. 175).
Seneca: cf. 'My Heart Goes Out' (p. 147).

Tom Snooks the Pundit, p. 168

(*Me Again*, p. 225. Undated.)
Cf. 'This writing business' (p. 106).

Scorpion and Other Poems

Scorpion, p. 169

'This night . . .': 'But God said unto him, Thou fool, this night thy soul shall be required of thee.' *Luke* 12:20.

In Kay Dick, *Ivy and Stevie*, p. 46: 'Did you see that poem I wrote, "Scorpion", in the *Nation* the other week? . . . Scorpion's got a new grievance—he's a wonderful animal, and his new grievance is that his soul has not been required of him . . . I do think it's beautiful. . . .'

How Do You See?, p. 169

Incorporates an earlier poem from *The Frog Prince* (1966) 'Oh Christianity, Christianity', which goes from 'Oh Christianity, Christianity' (p. 172) to 'You never answer our questions' (p. 173).
'the verse in Mark': 'I have heard it said that the verse "His blood be on us

and on our children", a verse from which has derived so much cruel persecution, is not authentic.' (*Me Again*, p. 160.)
'Their shifty theology of birth control': one of the main topics of debate at the 2nd Vatican Council, under Pope John XXIII, 1962–5.

The argument of this poem is treated at length in the essay 'Some Impediments to Christian Commitment' (1968), *Me Again*, pp. 153–70. *Collected Poems* has 'fresh air' in line 22.

Nor We Of Her To Him, p. 174
Cf. Lewis Carroll, *Alice's Adventures in Wonderland*, chapter XII:

> They told me you had been to her,
> And mentioned me to him:
> She gave me a good character,
> But said I could not swim.

Oh grateful colours, bright looks!, p. 175
Cf. 'What Poems are Made Of' (p. 168).

Reading this poem (BBC recording 29 November 1968) she comments on 'the pagan idea of death—the idea you get in the *Iliad* of the poor ghosts having to drink blood'. Cf. 'Persephone' (p. 114), note.

Archie and Tina, p. 175
Cf. *The Holiday*, p. 122: 'I remember the long summer days of childhood that are such a pleasure, nothing is ever such a pleasure again, tired and hot and happy the hours come to teatime.'

Reading this poem (BBC recording 29 November 1968) she comments: 'A very happy poem ... I love the East Coast so much. [This is] about fifty years ago, of course.'

The House of Over-Dew, p. 177
In Kay Dick, *Ivy and Stevie*, p. 48: 'The chapter [in *The Holiday*] which is called Over Dew had been a short story, but I couldn't get it published. I think it's very beautiful. Well, not very long ago I was reading this thing, and I thought, "This is not prose, it falls into verse," and I said, "If it doesn't fall into verse I'm going to help it." So I copied it out again and sold it as a poem, "The House of Over-Dew" ... I don't know whether to call it Overdew, which suggests it's rather a long time coming along, or Over-dew which suggests rising damp.'

In *The Holiday*, pp. 177–81, the story occurs in the context of Celia's thoughts about Tennyson's *Maud* ('dignity in suffering', 'the simple noble way of going wrong') compared to 'our modern love stories'. '*Maud* is wild, and this is nervous.' But, in the knowledge of what the Nazis have done ('the maximum of pain with the maximum of indignity') Tennyson's dignified suffering seems to us 'absurd'. 'So I thought after all there might be truth in my story and the sap of strife and life.'

To give an idea of the kinds of small changes Stevie Smith made when she turned the story from prose into verse, I give verse 6 in its prose form: The *Over-Dew* idea was orthodox Christian. When Mr Minnim retired from his accountancy work he said that they should move from the suburb where they lived and buy the house of *Over-Dew*, which was a retreat for missionaries to have on their leave holidays in England. But now it was being run, he said, in a fantastical fashion. When they bought it everything would be different, and better. Where was the money to come from? No matter. They had their savings, also they had the faith of Mr and Mrs Minnim. Mrs Minnim loved her husband and was proud of him and pleased to follow him to the end of the world. And certainly *Over-Dew* was not that.

Greats: Classics.

St Benedict: Italian monk who held strongly to the celibate life and whose order, the Benedictines, follow the rule of implicit obedience, celibacy, abstaining from laughter, spare diet, poverty, the exercise of hospitality, observance of feastdays, fasts, and unremitting industry.

'a Latin prayer': the 'devotio'. A Roman general, if the battle went against him, could devote himself to the 'Manes' (spirits of the dead), and seek death at the hands of the enemy. If he was not then killed, he could never sacrifice to the gods again. (Livy, *History of Rome*, 8.9.4ff.)

Hendecasyllables, p. 182

'Hendecasyllables': 11-syllabic lines. In Stevie Smith's selection for the *Batsford Book of Children's Verse*, she includes Coleridge's 'Catullan Hendecasyllables', which she quotes from in *The Holiday*, p. 46. Cf. also Tennyson's experiments in classical metres, including 'Hendecasyllabics', 'All composed in a metre of Catullus'.

'It is the very bewitching hour . . .': ' "Tis now the very witching time of night', *Hamlet*, III, ii, 413.

'On Writing', p. 185

These quotations are taken from the following sources: *Me Again* (*MA*); Kay Dick, *Ivy and Stevie* (*IS*); and *Over the Frontier* (*OTF*):

IS, p. 48; *MA*, p. 353; *MA*, p. 268; *MA*, p. 104; *MA* p. 149; *MA*, p. 119; *MA*, p. 181; *OTF*, p. 66; *MA*, p. 127; *MA*, p. 256; *MA*, p. 335; *MA*, p. 290; *MA*, p. 280; *MA*, p. 298; *IS*, p. 44; *MA*, p. 297; *MA* p. 128; *IS*, p. 44; *MA*, p. 283; *MA*, p. 345.

Index of Titles

———————————— ✳ ————————————

Index of First Lines

————————————————— ✳ —————————————————